CABINET OF CURIOSITIES

COLLECTING AND UNDERSTANDING THE WONDERS OF THE NATURAL WORLD

GORDON GRICE

WORKMAN PUBLISHING • NEW YORK

For Tracy, Parker, Beckett, Griffin, and Abby

Library of Congress Cataloging-in-Publication Data is available.

ISBN 978-0-7611-6927-7

Cover design by Raquel Jaramillo and Colleen AF Venable
Interior design by Raquel Jaramillo and Gordon Whiteside
Front cover photo by Raquel Jaramillo
Back cover photos: Picsfive/Shutterstock.com (vintage papers);
Bertrand Benoit/CGtextures (wood background); Dover Publications, Inc.
(octopus and beetle)
Photo research by Raquel Jaramillo
For additional photo and art credits, please see page 188,
which constitutes a continuation of the copyright page.

Workman books are available at special discounts when purchased in bulk for premiums and sales promotions as well as for fund-raising or educational use. Special editions or book excerpts can also be created to specification. For details, contact the Special Sales Director at the address below or send an email to specialmarkets@workman.com.

Workman Publishing Company, Inc.
225 Varick Street
New York, NY 10014–4381
workman.com

WORKMAN is a registered trademark of Workman Publishing Co., Inc.

Printed in China
First printing September 2015

10 9 8 7 6 5 4 3 2 1

CONTENTS

1   **INTRODUCTION:** My First Cabinet

14   **PART ONE:** Classifying Life on Earth {How to Organize All Living Things}
17   **CHAPTER ONE:** Classification

34   **PART TWO:** Animalia {The Animal Kingdom}
37   **CHAPTER TWO:** Phylum Chordata
77   **CHAPTER THREE:** Phylum Arthropoda
125   **CHAPTER FOUR:** Phylum Mollusca
135   **CHAPTER FIVE:** Phyla Echinodermata, Cnidaria, and Porifera

144   **PART THREE:** Plantae {The Plant Kingdom}
147   **CHAPTER SIX:** Divisions Magnoliophyta, Pinophyta, Ginkgophyta, and Lycophyta

162   **PART FOUR:** Mineralium
165   **CHAPTER SEVEN:** Minerals, Gemstones, and Rocks (Plus Fossils)

182   **AFTERWORD:** Curiosities

187   **ACKNOWLEDGMENTS**
187   **ABOUT THE AUTHOR**
188   **PHOTO AND ART CREDITS**

MY FIRST CABINET

When I was about six, I started my first cabinet of curiosities. The first thing I put in it was a skunk's skull I found in our backyard. The skull fit perfectly in my palm. It had sharp little teeth. I was surprised to notice that they looked like my dogs', with long, jagged canines on the sides. Without its lips, the skull seemed stuck in a snarl. Fur still clung to it—black with a stripe of white down the forehead.

I put the skull in a red cigar box my dad gave me. The box was made of sturdy cardboard with a hinged lid. I was soon using it to collect all sorts of things I found outdoors, from old coins to corncobs.

Over the years I found many items to add to my cigar box. One day our dogs came home with porcupine quills stuck in their mouths and snouts. They had fought a porcupine and lost. My dad pulled the quills out with pliers and gave them to me. They were about the size of toothpicks. The stuff they

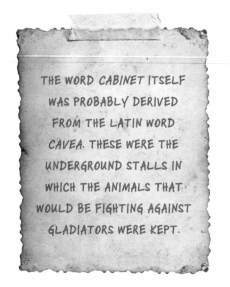

THE WORD CABINET ITSELF WAS PROBABLY DERIVED FROM THE LATIN WORD CAVEA. THESE WERE THE UNDERGROUND STALLS IN WHICH THE ANIMALS THAT WOULD BE FIGHTING AGAINST GLADIATORS WERE KEPT.

were made of felt like fingernails. Into my cigar box they went. Another time, my sister and I found some wooden seed pods called devil's claws. Into the box they went. When my pet tarantula died, into the box he went.

That cigar box became my first cabinet of curiosities. I didn't call it that at the time. I only learned that term later.

THE AGE OF EXPLORATION

People have been keeping collections like the one I started in my cigar box for more than two thousand years. In ancient times, collections of curiosities were kept in temples. In the city of Carthage, for example, the temple for the goddess Astarte was said to house many strange things for people to look at—even the skin of a chimpanzee. A whalebone was displayed in the temple of Asclepius in Sicyon, and a temple in Naples kept an elephant skull. In ancient Rome, temples held vast collections of curiosities from all over the empire, plus paintings, sculptures, jewelry, and books. (In those days, books were rare and extremely valuable.)

It wasn't until much later that collections started to be kept in special cabinets. Nowadays, we think of cabinets as pieces of furniture. Kitchen cabinets. Toy cabinets. Storage cabinets. Basically, any piece of furniture that has shelves, or drawers, and maybe doors is called a cabinet. But the word *cabinet* goes back to the Middle Ages. In France, a cabinet was a "small room." In time it came to mean any place where things are stored, and it could be as small as my cigar box or as big as a house. In fact, some cabinets took up several buildings—and were the basis of what later became known as museums.

Cabinets started becoming really popular during the the Age of Exploration. This was a time between the early 1400s and the late 1600s when people from Europe began sailing to other places in the world, such as Africa, Asia, Australia, the Pacific Islands, and the Americas. They went to these places to make money and discover new things. In a way, the term "Age of Exploration" is misleading. All of those places had already been explored by the people who lived there. But the places were new to Europeans.

The Europeans brought back valuable things, like gold, silver, and spices. They also brought back things they found curious, like animals and plants they had never seen before, rocks and gemstones, fossils, and bones. Some Europeans, especially

This engraving from Ferrante Imperato's *Dell'historia naturale* (Naples, 1599) depicts one of the earliest known natural history collections in Europe.

Jacob Hoefnagel, the court painter in Prague from 1602 to 1613, rendered this likeness of a dodo bird said to be preserved in Rudolf II's collection. The dodo bird is now extinct.

wealthy ones, collected these rare finds and built cabinets to hold them. Their main purpose was to not only catalog the strange and exotic wonders of the world, but to learn about the earth and be able to show other people what they'd learned.

Those old-time cabinets held many things: human heads and horseshoe nails, sheet music and meteorites, stuffed birds and animal skins, fruits, seeds, tools, and more. The collection of Rudolf II was said to have a stuffed dodo bird. Another collection had an ostrich egg. A third had the skull of the collector's favorite composer. These cabinets could house dozens or hundreds of "curiosities," depending on how big they were—and some got very big. A powerful prince named William of Orange had a huge cabinet of curiosities. He even kept a live orangutan in it!

Kings, popes, and other powerful people tried to get as many curiosities as they could. Sometimes they hired ship captains to bring back interesting things from the lands they visited. In that way, they collected not just strange animals and plants, but also things dug up from the earth: fossils, gems, interesting rocks. They also found items made by native peoples in those distant regions. Bowls, arrowheads, sewing needles made of bone. These man-made curiosities, whether they came from newly discovered tribes in America or nomads in Africa, were highly sought after and often hard-won. Treasure hunters abounded, looking not only for gold and silver, but also for rare artifacts to sell to wealthy collectors.

Some people were dishonest. Instead of finding or buying weird animals, they made fake ones and pretended they were real. For example, they would sew together parts of a monkey and a fish to make a mermaid. They would glue fake parts onto a dead rat and call it a baby dragon. They would make a basilisk (a monster from old myths that could kill you by just breathing on you) by sewing claws and a snake tongue into a dead stingray. Collectors believed they were really seeing these monsters!

Sometimes people weren't trying to fake anything. They just misunderstood what they had. For example, in the late 1500s, a king named Ferdinand of Habsburg was said to have the bones of genuine "giants" in his cabinet. People really believed that a gigantic race of humans had once walked the earth, and that a huge flood had killed them all. But the bones in Ferdinand of Habsburg's cabinet were not giant human bones at all. They were really dinosaur bones.

Much of what we know about the natural world came from cabinets of curiosities. Take fossils, for example. When people started digging up thousands of fossils for cabinets, they discovered something important: The different layers of earth hold different kinds of fossils. People found modern-looking plants and seashells at one level. At a deeper level, they found different species of plants and different kinds of shells. This insight eventually led scientists to grasp that the earth is billions of years old. They realized that deeper layers are older and contain older animals and plants. They can look at layers 70 million years old and find the bones of dinosaurs like T. rex and triceratops. We can look at deeper layers from 150 million years ago and discover the bones of stegosaurus and apatosaurus. They now know that the earth is still evolving today.

The field of medicine owes much to cabinets of curiosity, as well. Many cabinet collectors were not only interested in the biology and anatomy of creatures from around the world, but were also fascinated by human biology. Although it might seem kind of morbid to us nowadays, many collections were filled with skulls and skeletons of people. This was one way doctors were able to learn about the human body. Frederik Ruysch, a prominent Dutch physician in the 17th century, actually performed dissections in front of students and spectators so that they could learn the basics of medicine. Then he would create decorative curiosity collections using human skeletons from his autopsies.

Drawing of a diorama from Frederik Ruysch's anatomical curiosity collection. These dioramas were often made from human parts.

The Cabinet of Ole Worm (1588-1655)

Ole Worm (seriously, that was his name) was a doctor, an artist, a philosopher, and a teacher of Latin, Greek, physics, and medicine. Although he lived primarily in Denmark, he traveled extensively and corresponded with people all over the world. Sometimes they sent him items for his cabinet, which he meticulously drew in order to catalog his collection. Worm had thousands of birds, reptiles, fish, minerals, and other things in his cabinet. Some of the more famous items in Worm's collection are listed below.

- **A shark.** He hung it from the ceiling with ropes. Like most of his animal specimens, it had been preserved through taxidermy, its flesh removed through an incision in the belly and replaced with sawdust before mounting.

- **Antlers from deer.** In some cases, he had the skull or even the whole head hanging on the wall of his cabinet. In other cases, it was just the antlers.

- **Shells from giant tortoises.** These tortoises can grow to four feet long and weigh more than 600 pounds. Some of them are big enough for kids to ride on their backs.

- **The bill from a sawfish.** A sawfish's bill, or snout, is shaped like a saw with teeth on both sides. The sawfish uses it to stir up clams, fish, and other prey hiding in the mud on the ocean floor.

- **A squid.**

- **Rocks made of a mineral called sulfur.**

- **The skull of a male narwhal.** A narwhal is a kind of whale. One of its teeth grows into a tusk as long as ten feet. It looks like a horn. Nobody knows what this tusk is for. It might somehow help the narwhal sense things under water. Or it might make

him attractive to female narwhals. People used to think these tusks came from unicorns. Worm did not believe in unicorns. He proved that the so-called unicorn horns really came from narwhals.

- **A nine-banded armadillo.** This little mammal, about the size of a football, has a tough, leathery shell to protect it. It waddles around at night, digging for bugs to eat.

- **A spoonbill.** This is a bird that wades in the water. It uses its wide, flat bill to scoop up crustaceans and other food.

The Herbarium of the Duchess of Beaufort (1630–1714)

Mary Somerset, Duchess of Beaufort, liked to garden. She didn't just grow plants, however. She also collected them, had them dried, and pasted them into books. Although she lived in England in the 1600s, she had much more than plants just from England and the British Isles in her collection. She had more than 1,500 specimens brought in from places as far away as India, China, and South Africa.

When she could, she would put in the entire plant in the book. She did that with a dogbane plant, for instance. Dogbane plants have pointy leaves, clusters of little white flowers, and a sap that's sticky and white. She dried the dogbane, knowing its sap would rot inside her book if she didn't, and preserved the plant in its entirety.

Sometimes she would only put in a part of a plant, especially if the plant was too big to fit inside her book. That's why she only put in four leafy branches of the caper bush, which can grow to more than a yard tall and a yard wide. Each leaf was thick and shaped like a thumbprint. This kind of collection—dried plants gathered in a book—is called a herbarium. The duchess eventually made twelve big herbariums. She left her collection to a man named Sir Hans Sloane.

The Cabinet of Hans Sloane (1660–1753)

Sir Hans Sloane had one of the biggest curiosity collections in the world. Born in Ireland in 1660, he began collecting specimens from nature as a child, which led him to develop a keen interest in science. He became a physician and moved to England, where his collection continued to grow. He was said to have 5,843 different seashells, for instance—all cataloged and documented. In time, he began to collect other people's collections, which he either bought or received as donations from people who knew he would take good care of them. How did all that stuff fit into a cabinet? Well, it didn't! He had many, many cabinets inside many, many rooms. Hans's curiosity collection was so big, in fact, that after he died, the British government used it as the foundation for the British Museum, one of the world's largest museums dedicated to natural and human history.

The Cabinet of Manfredo Settala (1600–1680)

Manfredo Settala built clocks, compasses, and microscopes, so it's not surprising he liked to include delicate instruments in his collection. He inherited a cabinet of curiosities from his father and spent his life adding to it. Besides scientific gadgets, he collected skeletons, rocks, weapons, pressed leaves, paintings, and much more. His most amazing find happened when a monk died under mysterious circumstances at a monastery in his hometown of Milan, Italy. The monk was killed by a stone that fell on him from the sky. Settala explained that the stone was a meteorite—a piece of space debris that fell to earth. He put the meteor in his cabinet.

Cabinet of Artefacts and Curiosities (1695–present)

August Hermann Francke (1663–1727) began his collection partly as a way of teaching kids at the orphanage where he worked. More than a century later, an artist and naturalist named Gottfried August Gründler cataloged Francke's collection and made cabinets for it. Some of the students at the orphanage grew up to be missionaries. Many of them sent curiosities from their travels back to the orphanage. In that way, the collection grew for centuries. It still exists today.

SPECIAL KINDS OF CABINETS

Over the years, I added many things to my cigar box cabinet. I put in insects, fossils, shells, seeds, and lots of other items that interested me. I had some problems with some of the objects I put in there, though. Take the tarantula, for instance. It eventually dried up and broke into pieces—its legs came off, and the two sections of its body broke apart. Finally, it was such a mess that I threw away everything except its fangs. Those stayed attached to each other, and I could take them out to show my friends whenever I wanted. I wish I'd known back then how to preserve a spider. I could have kept that tarantula whole for years!

In time my collection became too big to keep in the cigar box. For a long time, I used a big shelf in my room as my "cabinet." Nowadays I use a whole room in my basement. Whenever I find a cicada shell or a plant leaf that I want to study, I take it home and put it in my cabinet.

My oldest son has a cabinet of his own, too. He calls it "The Box of Weirdness." He likes to fill it with curiosities he finds when he goes for walks. It contains an old snakeskin, a big pinecone, a metal spring that was probably part of a car, and a weird-shaped piece of tree bark.

Photos from the author's own curiosity cabinet

The point is, anyone can have a cabinet of curiosity, and I think everyone should. You can put whatever you like in your own cabinet. It can be a lifetime project, like the one I keep in my basement, or just a short-time project, like a hometown cabinet I started a few years ago.

The last time I went to my hometown, which I hadn't been to in many years, I decided to collect a few curiosities that would remind me of where I grew up, such as:

- A spider's egg sac
- Seed pods from a yucca plant
- Part of a branch from a red cedar tree, with its blue fruit attached
- Hard little berries from a weed called horse nettle
- A piece of tree bark with green lichen on it
- A dried leaf from an iris my grandmother planted
- The egg case of a mantis
- Flowers from a thistle
- A stick from a rosebush my mom planted
- The tip of an elm tree branch with buds on it
- A snake's rattle (just like the one I had when I was a kid)

I saw many other plants and animals on my trip home, but these were the ones I chose for my hometown cabinet collection because they were the best reminders of my hometown. They represent a lot of the things you can find there. For example, there are lots of yucca plants where I grew up. The main thing you see when you look at a yucca is a lot of long, prickly leaves, plus maybe a woody stalk with some seed pods on it. The leaves are like spears pointing in every direction. They protect the plant from being eaten by animals. Yuccas grow where it is dry, which is why they have deep roots: so they can suck up water from far below the ground. Every place is home to plants and animals that thrive in its particular temperature, humidity, and terrain. So for me, the yucca plant was very representative of my hometown.

You can make your cabinet be about anything you want: all of natural history or one special kind of collection. Do you like bugs or bones? Flowers or butterflies? Do you want to collect only things you can find in your neighborhood? Or would you like to have people from other places send you interesting stuff? Or do you just want to put in anything you like? It's up to you.

WHERE TO FIND A CABINET FOR YOUR COLLECTION

What sort of cabinet should you use? It kind of depends on the size of your collection. Here are some possibilities to get your imagination going:

Fishing tackle boxes or artist's storage boxes. These can be made of metal or plastic and have small compartments. Sometimes the compartments are arranged in drawers that fold up when you shut the box.

A plastic storage box made for screws, nuts, and bolts. These have little compartments that are ideal for collecting seeds, rocks, and other small items.

A desk organizer. Almost any stationery store carries one of these handy tray inserts. You can use just one if you have a small collection, or you can hang a few up next to one another to create a large display.

A shoebox. You can cut the cover of the shoebox into strips that you then tape or glue inside the box to make compartments. If the shoebox has logos or writing on it, you can paint it white or wrap it in brown kraft paper.

A cigar box. This, as I mentioned earlier, was what I used for my first cabinet of curiosities. It's a great option for everyone.

A pizza box. First, make sure the box has been thoroughly cleaned. Then, either use the box lid to create compartments or cut strips of cardboard from another box.

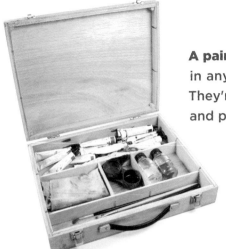

A painter's box. These beautiful wooden suitcases, which can be found in any arts and crafts store, come with compartments already built in. They're also usually unfinished wood, which means you can get creative and paint them inside and out.

An old library card cabinet. These cabinets full of little drawers are very reminiscent of some of the original curiosity cabinets.

A printer's or typesetter's box. Years ago, typesetters used something called a letterpress to print things, and they set all the type by hand using little metal alphabet blocks. These alphabet blocks were kept inside huge printer's boxes. When people started using computers to set type in the 1980s, this method of printing went out of use. Printers discarded these wooden boxes, but you can still find them in vintage and antique stores. If you do see one, grab it—these make the best display cases for your collectibles.

A DVD or CD storage shelf—or even a small bookcase. This is also a good option if you have a collection full of larger objects. A good craft store will have lightweight balsa wood that you can cut down to create smaller compartments on each shelf.

Small wooden crates or soda bottle cases. Farmers' markets and fruit stands are a good place to find wooden crates, as fruits and vegetables are often transported in these kinds of boxes. Soda bottle cases are harder to come by, since they were used decades ago to store soda bottles, but you can still find them in flea markets and thrift stores. Hang these boxes up next to one another on a wall to create a dazzling display. You can do the same with shoeboxes and cardboard boxes, by the way. This is a really great option if you have a lot of wall space and if you have big items in your collection.

HOW TO BUILD YOUR OWN CABINET

If you can't find a printer's box or any of the other items on the preceding pages, you can always make your own cabinet. It's not hard, and doesn't require any hammering or sawing, and uses supplies easily found in any arts and crafts store.

WHAT YOU NEED:

- One 12" x 24" painting panel (You'll be using the back of the panel, not the front.)
- Five ¼" x 1 ½" x 36" balsa wood panels
- Glue (must dry clear)
- Scissors or X-ACTO knife (Use with caution.)
- Ruler

1. Measure the width of the interior of the back frame of the painting panel. This is going to be the base of your cabinet. Carefully cut five pieces of balsa wood to create the horizontal shelves. You can either cut the balsa wood with an X-ACTO knife or scissors.

2. Apply glue along the length and sides of the balsa wood.

3. Gently wedge the balsa piece onto the panel between the side of the frame. Hold for a few minutes to let glue set a little. Straighten by eye or using ruler. The shelf should be perpendicular to the side of the frame.

4. Apply extra glue wherever shelves and panel meet. Wait for glue to dry.

5. Repeat step 3 with the other shelves, depending on how many you want. Make sure the shelves are parallel to one another—and perpendicular to the sides.

6. To attach vertical dividers to your cabinet, measure the distance between the horizontal shelves. Cut the balsa wood to that size. Add glue and insert the vertical pieces. Repeat to attach all the vertical dividers on your cabinet. Allow glue to dry overnight.

7. After your cabinet is finished, you can leave it natural, stain, or paint it. If you decide to stain or paint it, sand it down first to remove any glue residue.

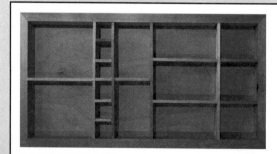

WHAT YOU CAN LEARN IN THIS BOOK

In this book, I include tips for how to preserve many of the things you might collect, from leaves to butterflies. I'll also suggest some things to look for. You don't have to use any of these suggestions, but you might have fun looking through the ideas anyway. This book isn't just a list of suggestions, though. In it, you'll find out interesting facts about how these items fit into the natural world. Where do they come from? Where do they lay their eggs? What do they eat? As you learn the answers to questions like these, you will begin to see that everything in the world is connected. Those connections are what science is all about.

Science is an attempt to find out how the world fits together. Scientists observe, describe, and identify things in the physical world. They experiment to find out more about these items; they develop theories to explain relationships among them. All scientists work according to certain rules. For example, they work toward objective information instead of opinions. As part of being objective, they prize information that can be replicated—that is, found separately by different observers. For instance, if one person reports seeing a new kind of animal, he might just be mistaken. But if fifty different people say they have seen this animal, scientists consider the information much more valuable. It has been replicated by different observers. Scientists aren't satisfied until such an animal has actually been examined by people from all around the world. Replication is key.

It all begins with looking at the item with careful attention. A cabinet is a great tool for observation because it allows you to gather items to examine whenever you want to. You may look at a specimen long after you first collected it and make an exciting discovery—a subtle color pattern in a shell, say, or a resemblance between an old skull and one you've just found. The cabinet gives you many chances to observe an item at different times and in different frames of mind. If you give it a chance, it will stoke your imagination.

I hope your cabinet will make you curious to learn more. Curiosity is what makes it a cabinet and not just a box of stuff.

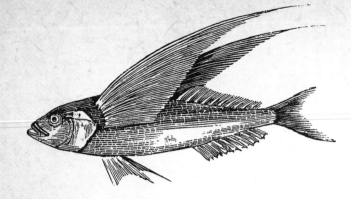

PART ONE

CLASS

LIFE ON

{HOW TO ORGANIZE

FYING
EARTH

ALL LIVING THINGS}

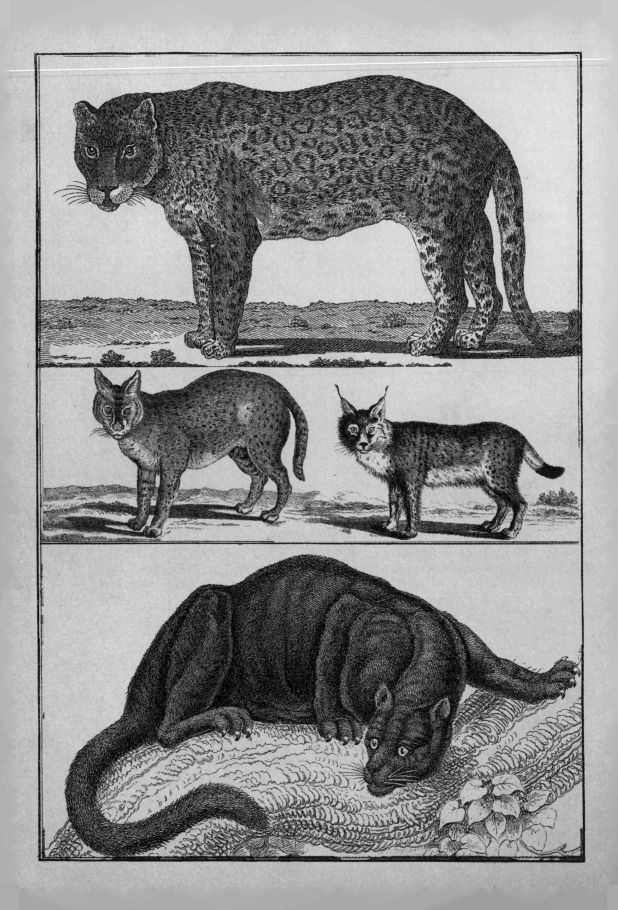

CHAPTER ONE

CLASSIFICATION

Question: What's the difference between a mountain lion and a cougar?

Answer: Nothing. Those are different English words for the same animal.

Common names for organisms can be confusing. For example, if you read about an Argentine ranch where the cattle are sometimes attacked by *el tigre*, you might picture a big catlike animal with stripes, because *tigre* sounds like the English word *tiger*. But it actually means jaguar—a different catlike animal with spots on its amber coat.

When it comes to common names, people can call organisms whatever makes sense to them, depending on where they live and what animals live there. For example, European Americans who settled in the Appalachian Mountains called the cougar a *panther* because it resembled an Old World animal that was called a *panther*. They didn't have to worry about confusing the two, because only one occurred in their new home.

But scientists need to be more precise, because they have to communicate clearly with other researchers across the globe. They use a system of scientific names—a taxonomy. This is the science of grouping biological organisms by common characteristics, and giving names to the groups. The system that is still being used today is based on a system invented by a Swedish biologist named Carl Linnaeus (1707–1778). Linnaeus set up a standard set of names for living things, which he then ranked. He wanted them to be understood by scientists everywhere, so he didn't use Swedish, English, or other languages spoken in particular countries. Instead, he based his names on Latin and Greek, two ancient languages read by educated people in many different countries.

Linnaeus's system grouped organisms into smaller and smaller sets to show which creatures are similar to each other. Later, scientists refined his system. And even now the system for classifying living things is still changing as scientists learn new things about how different organisms are related. They're also still discovering new organisms and life-forms. Despite all the modifications, however, the basic system of classification still follows Linnaeus's method of categorizing life.

Linnaeus believed that the world was divided into three kingdoms—animal, vegetable, and mineral. Although life on earth has proven to be much more complicated than that, it's not a bad way to organize a cabinet of curiosity—and it's a great way to organize this book!

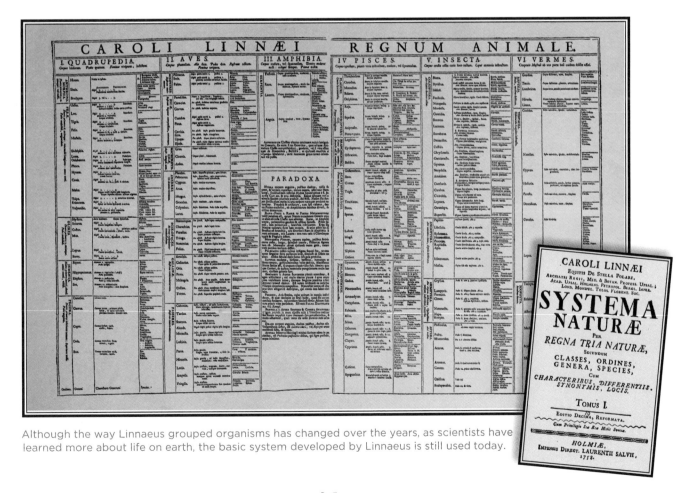

Although the way Linnaeus grouped organisms has changed over the years, as scientists have learned more about life on earth, the basic system developed by Linnaeus is still used today.

TAXONOMIC RANKS

There are eight major taxonomic ranks. In between these rankings scientists sometimes put subcategories, but the main system of biological classification divides life on earth into these eight ranks.

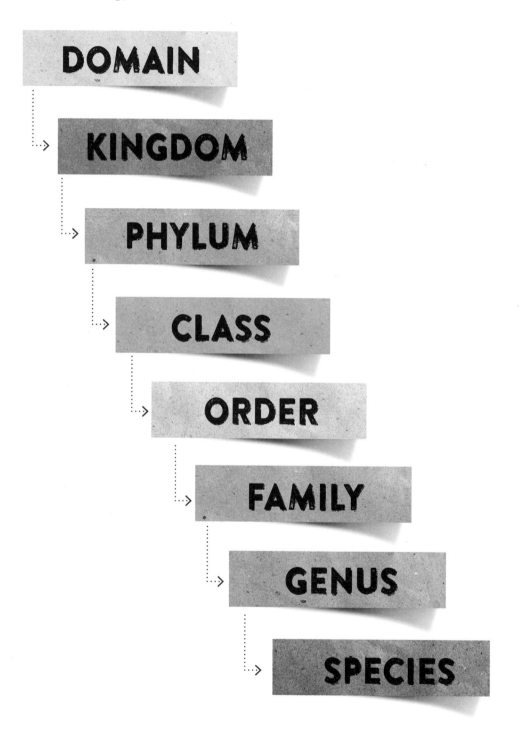

DOMAIN

KINGDOM

PHYLUM

CLASS

ORDER

FAMILY

GENUS

SPECIES

DOMAIN

According to one current version of Linnaeus's system, all life on earth is divided into two categories, which are called **domains**. One domain is called **Eukaryota**. It contains most of the living things you could think of—plants, animals, and more. All of these organisms are made of cells that contain at least one nucleus. (A nucleus is the control center of the cell, where the DNA is located.)

The other domain is **Prokaryota**. It contains organisms whose cells don't have a fully formed nucleus. Mostly they are single-celled organisms like bacteria. Another example of a prokaryote is blue-green algae—some species of it form the scum often found floating on ponds. Prokaryotes aren't usually easy to identify or collect, so we'll focus on eukaryotes in this book.

KINGDOM

Scientists are currently trying to figure out and name the **kingdoms** in the domain Eukaryota. Most of them comprise microscopic life-forms that don't interest us for collecting. The three most easily observed kingdoms are these:

Kingdom: Animalia
The animals

Kingdom: Plantae
The plants

Kingdom: Fungi
Mushrooms, molds, and their relatives

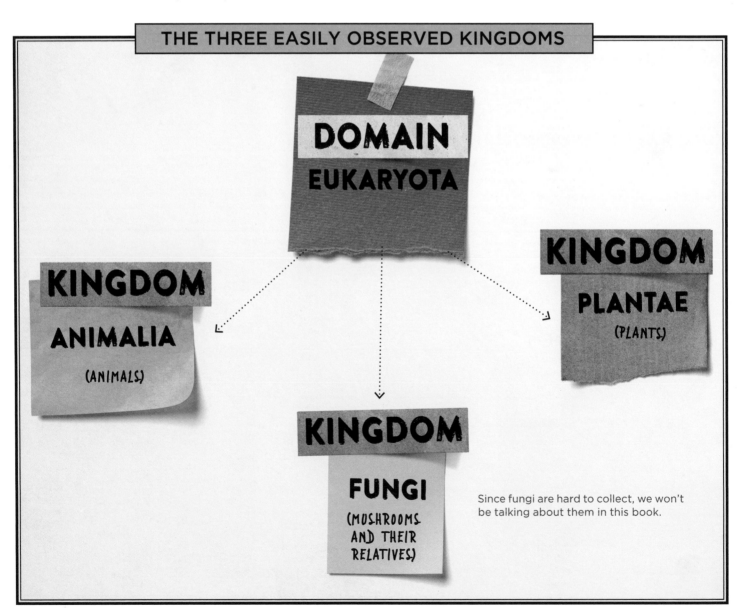

THE THREE EASILY OBSERVED KINGDOMS

DOMAIN
EUKARYOTA

KINGDOM
ANIMALIA
(ANIMALS)

KINGDOM
PLANTAE
(PLANTS)

KINGDOM
FUNGI
(MUSHROOMS
AND THEIR
RELATIVES)

Since fungi are hard to collect, we won't be talking about them in this book.

PHYLUM

The next level of classification is called **phylum**. There are approximately thirty-five phyla in the animal kingdom and twelve phyla in the plant kingdom, though those numbers are constantly being revised as scientists learn new things about different organisms. For the purposes of this book, though, I'm only listing the most commonly encountered phyla. Most collectible things, with the exception of rocks and gems, will come from animals and plants on these lists.

Let's start with what is arguably the most collectible kingdom. Within the animal kingdom are all the animals that live now or have ever lived. Here are six common phyla:

Phylum: Chordata
These animals all have one thing in common: a long, hollow central nerve (a notochord) going down their backs. Most of the chordates are also vertebrates; that means their notochord is encased in a column of bone (a spine). Examples of chordates are fish, amphibians, reptiles, birds, and mammals.

Phylum: Arthropoda
All the animals in the phylum Arthropoda have movable limbs and an exoskeleton. They also have nervous, circulatory, reproductive, and digestive systems. Some examples of arthropods are insects, spiders, and crabs.

Phylum: Mollusca
Mollusks are animals with soft bodies that sometimes have shells. Examples of mollusks are slugs, snails, octopuses, squids, clams, oysters, and mussels.

Phylum: Annelida
Annelids are worms that have ringed or segmented bodies. One example is the earthworm.

Phylum: Cnidaria
Cnidarians have soft bodies without hard shells. They have no distinct front and back and often have tentacles that can sting. One example is the jellyfish.

Phylum: Echinodermata
Echinoderms live in the ocean or in tide pools, have internal skeletons, and often have limbs radiating from the center of their bodies. Examples are starfish and sea urchins.

SOME PHYLA OF THE ANIMAL KINGDOM

The animal kingdom is divided into many other phyla than appear here, but these are the most commonly encountered ones.

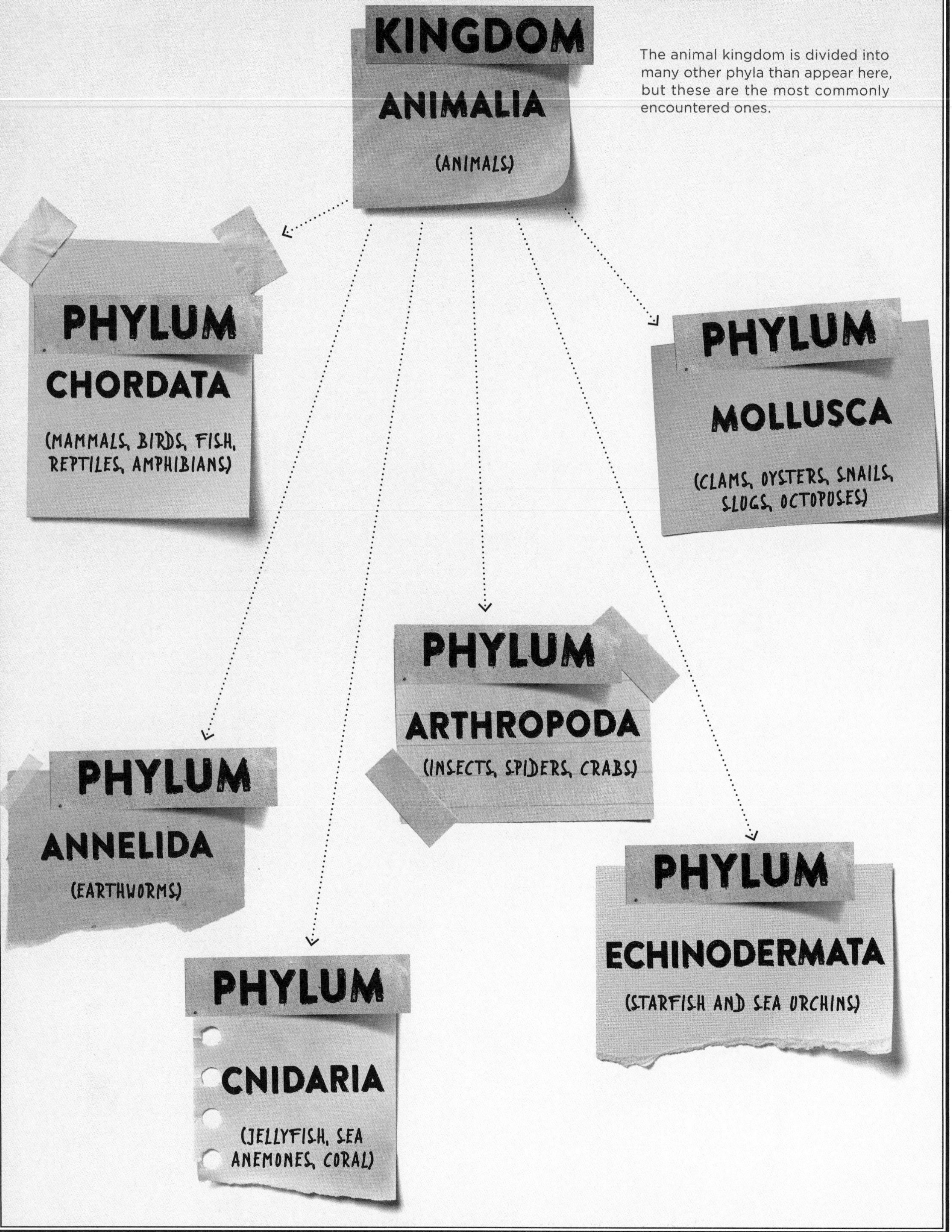
KINGDOM
ANIMALIA
(ANIMALS)
PHYLUM
CHORDATA
(MAMMALS, BIRDS, FISH, REPTILES, AMPHIBIANS)
PHYLUM
MOLLUSCA
(CLAMS, OYSTERS, SNAILS, SLUGS, OCTOPUSES)
PHYLUM
ARTHROPODA
(INSECTS, SPIDERS, CRABS)
PHYLUM
ANNELIDA
(EARTHWORMS)
PHYLUM
ECHINODERMATA
(STARFISH AND SEA URCHINS)
PHYLUM
CNIDARIA
(JELLYFISH, SEA ANEMONES, CORAL)

The plant kingdom is classified into twelve **divisions**, rather than phyla, based on things like how they reproduce, and their seed structure, form, and tissue structure. Here are four common divisions:

Division: Bryophyta
These plants are generally small and grow close to the ground. Most members of this division are called mosses. They are very important for the soil.

Division: Pteridophyta
These plants do not produce seeds but reproduce via spores. Examples are horsetails and ferns.

Division: Angiosperms
These are the flowering plants. Angiosperms produce seeds and reproduce through fertilization. Every tree that produces flowers is part of this phylum. Fruits and vegetables such as tomatoes, oranges, strawberries, grapes, and others fall into this division, too.

Division: Pinophyta
These plants are cone-bearing trees. Examples are redwoods, cedars, firs, pines, and spruces.

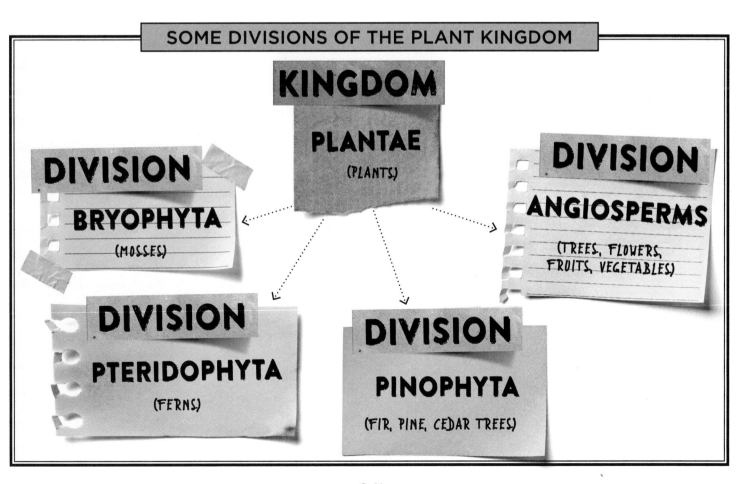

SOME DIVISIONS OF THE PLANT KINGDOM

KINGDOM
PLANTAE
(PLANTS)

DIVISION
BRYOPHYTA
(MOSSES)

DIVISION
PTERIDOPHYTA
(FERNS)

DIVISION
PINOPHYTA
(FIR, PINE, CEDAR TREES)

DIVISION
ANGIOSPERMS
(TREES, FLOWERS, FRUITS, VEGETABLES)

CLASS

Within each phylum are several **classes**. All the animals and plants within each class share characteristics that distinguish them from other animals and plants in their phylum. I'm not going to delve further into plant classes here, because that can get pretty technical, but I'm going to explain a little bit about some of the more common classes in the animal kingdom. Recognizing unique characteristics within classes may help you identify the curiosities you find.

In the phylum **Chordata**, there are fourteen classes, including these:

Class: Mammalia
Mammals share three traits not found in other chordates: They all have hair or fur; they all nurse their young; and they all have three bones in their middle ears. Some examples are dogs, elephants, and humans.

Class: Aves
Birds all share the following characteristics: They have feathers, wings, and bills. All birds lay eggs. Examples are eagles, sparrows, and toucans.

Class: Amphibia
Amphibians spend part of their lives in water and part on land. They lay eggs in layers of gel (not hard shells). Examples are frogs, toads, and salamanders.

Class: Reptilia
Reptiles have scales on their bodies and multi-boned lower jaws. Some examples are crocodiles, iguanas, and snakes.

Class: Chondrichthyes
These aquatic animals have skeletons made of cartilage (not bone) and teeth that are not attached to their jaws. Examples are sharks and rays.

Classes: Actinopterygii and Sarcopterygii
These classes include fish with skeletons made of bone. Some examples are tuna, trout, and catfish.

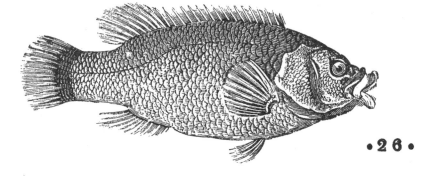

SOME CLASSES IN THE PHYLUM CHORDATA

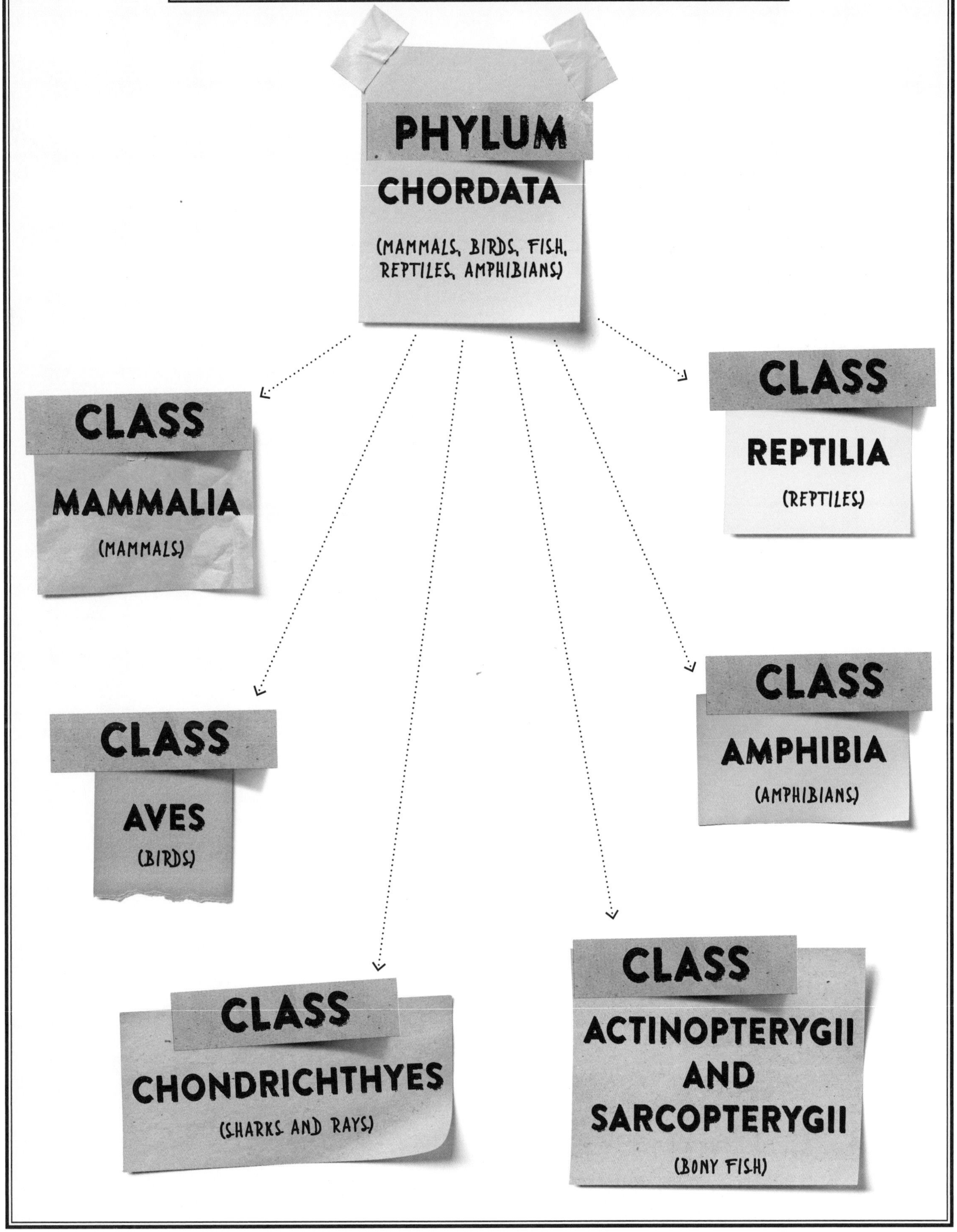
PHYLUM
CHORDATA
(MAMMALS, BIRDS, FISH, REPTILES, AMPHIBIANS)
CLASS
MAMMALIA
(MAMMALS)
CLASS
REPTILIA
(REPTILES)
CLASS
AVES
(BIRDS)
CLASS
AMPHIBIA
(AMPHIBIANS)
CLASS
CHONDRICHTHYES
(SHARKS AND RAYS)
CLASS
ACTINOPTERYGII AND SARCOPTERYGII
(BONY FISH)

In the phylum **Arthropoda**, there are fifteen classes. The best known include these:

Class: Insecta

Insects share the following characteristics: They have one pair of antennae, three pairs of legs, and three body sections. Some examples are beetles, flies, and moths.

Class: Arachnida

Animals in this class have no antennaes, four pairs of legs, and two body sections. Some examples are spiders, ticks, and scorpions.

Class: Chilopoda

Members of this class are called centipedes. Their long bodies are divided into many segments. Most of the segments have a pair of legs. The front pair of legs injects venom into prey.

Class: Diplopoda

Members of this class are called millipedes. Like centipedes, they have long bodies divided into many segments; but most millipedes' segments bear two pairs of legs.

Classes: Branchiopoda, Remipedia, Cephalocarida, Ostracoda, Malacostraca, and Maxillopoda

These classes are grouped as the crustaceans. Unique traits found in this group include branched limbs and a stage of development in which they use their antennae for swimming. Crustaceans are aquatic and have a hard exoskeleton and two pairs of antennae (though one pair is so small it is hard to see). Examples of crustaceans are shrimps crabs, and lobsters.

In the phylum **Mollusca**, there are nine classes, though I'm only listing the three that might be the most relevant to your collections.

Class: Bivalvia

Bivalves are animals with two shells. Some examples are clams, oysters, and mussels.

Class: Gastropoda

This class comprises snails and slugs.

Class: Cephalopoda

Cephalopods are aquatic animals with tentacles and large brains, such as squid, octopuses, and nautiluses.

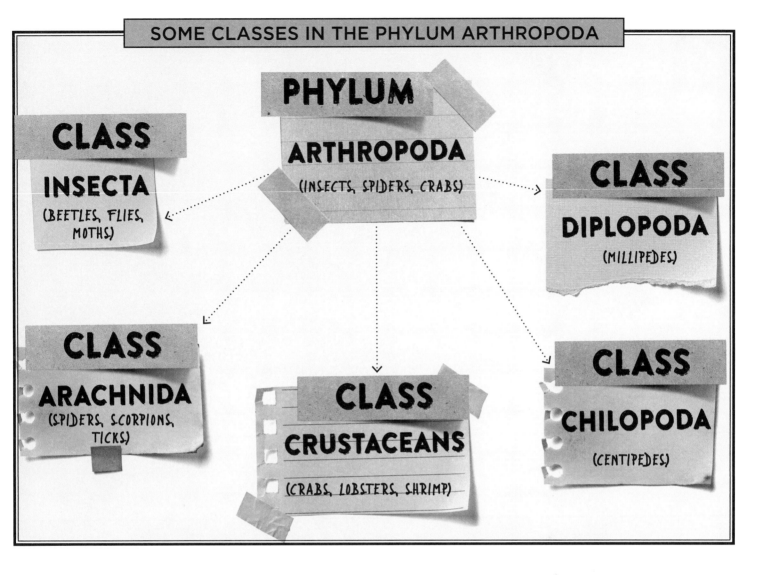

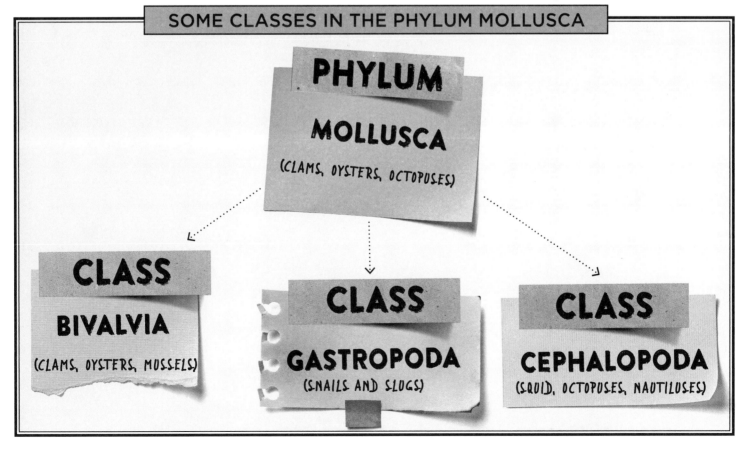

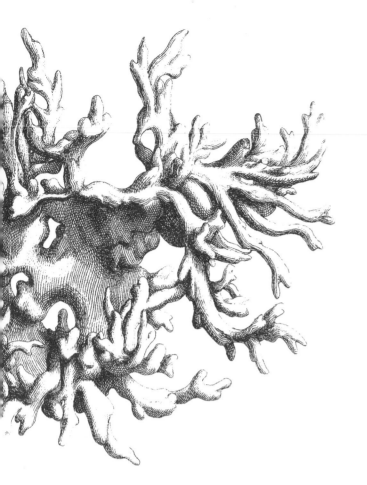

In the phylum **Cnidaria**, there are seven classes, including the four below:

Class: Anthozoa
This is the only class from which you might find a large assortment of collectibles, including sea anemones, sand dollars, and coral.

Class: Scyphozoa
This class includes true jellyfish.

Class: Hydrozoa
This class comprises the Portuguese man-of-war and hydras.

Class: Cubozoa
This class consists of box jellyfish.

In the phylum **Echinodermata** there are five classes.

Class: Asteroidea
This class comprises starfish. A starfish has five arms radiating from a central body.

Class: Crinoidea
Sea creatures in this class all have long, feathery arms radiating from a central body. An example is the sea lily.

Class: Ophiuroidea
These sea creatures, called brittle stars, have five snake-like arms radiating from a central body. Their arms are thinner than those of a starfish.

Class: Echinoidea
These sea creatures don't have arms, but may have many spines attached to their bodies. Sea urchins are an example of echinoids.

Class: Holothuroidea
Members of this class are called sea cucumbers. They have elongated cylindrical bodies and sometimes have tentacles.

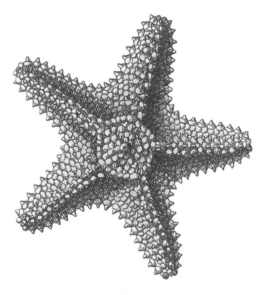

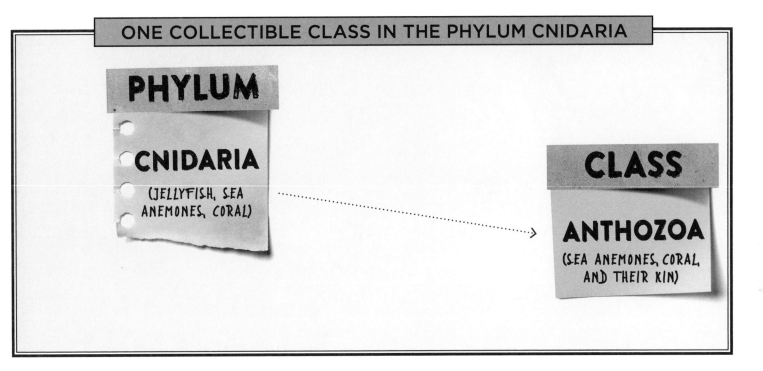

ONE COLLECTIBLE CLASS IN THE PHYLUM CNIDARIA

PHYLUM

CNIDARIA

(JELLYFISH, SEA ANEMONES, CORAL)

CLASS

ANTHOZOA

(SEA ANEMONES, CORAL, AND THEIR KIN)

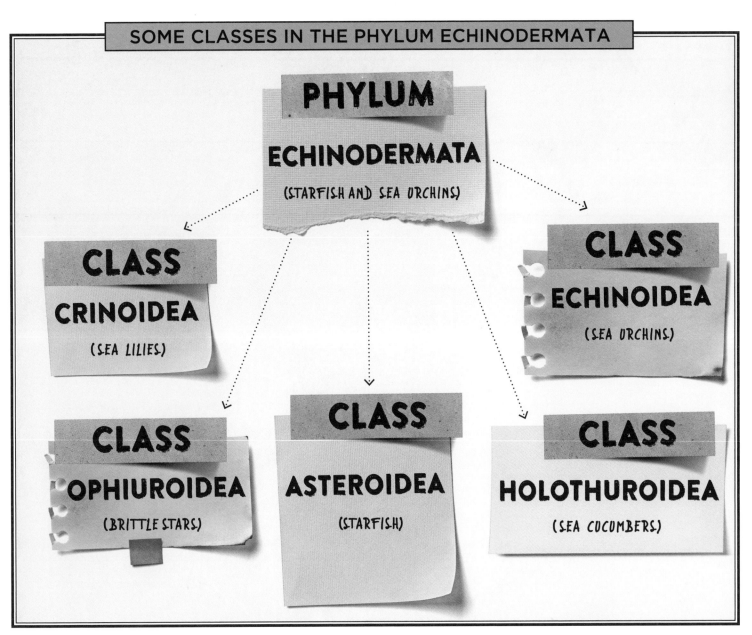

SOME CLASSES IN THE PHYLUM ECHINODERMATA

PHYLUM

ECHINODERMATA

(STARFISH AND SEA URCHINS)

CLASS

CRINOIDEA

(SEA LILIES)

CLASS

ECHINOIDEA

(SEA URCHINS)

CLASS

OPHIUROIDEA

(BRITTLE STARS)

CLASS

ASTEROIDEA

(STARFISH)

CLASS

HOLOTHUROIDEA

(SEA CUCUMBERS)

ORDER

Classes of animals are divided into **orders**. There are too many orders to discuss in detail in this chapter—or even to list. I'm only going to list the orders that may be of particular interest for the purposes of this book. You may find that many of your collectibles represent an animal from one of them.

COMMON ORDERS AMONG VARIOUS CLASSES

The following are some of the orders in the class Mammalia:

ORDER: PRIMATES
Mammals with large brains, flat nails, forward-facing eyes and stereoscopic vision, and mostly vertical posture, such as monkeys, apes, and humans

ORDER: DIDELPHIMORPHIA
Mammals whose females carry their young in pouches, such as opossums

ORDER: CHIROPTERA
Bats

ORDER: LAGOMORPHA
Rabbits and their kin

ORDER: RODENTIA
Mammals with ever-growing incisors, such as rats and squirrels. This is actually the largest order in the mammalian class: About 40 percent of all mammals belong to the order Rodentia.

ORDER: CARNIVORA
A mostly meat-eating group equipped with special jagged teeth for shearing meat. Examples are dogs, cats, and bears.

ORDER: ARTIODACTYLA
Mammals with cloven hooves, such as pigs, deer, and bison

The following are some of the orders in the class Aves:

ORDER: ANSERIFORMES
Aquatic birds, such as ducks, geese, and swans

ORDER: APODIFORMES
Birds with small feet and short legs that can't walk, such as hummingbirds and swifts

ORDER: CHARADRIIFORMES
Strong-flying birds, many of which fly or nest near open water, such as seagulls, sandpipers, and puffins

ORDER: CICONIIFORMES
Storks, which are long-legged, long-necked birds with strong bills

ORDER: COLUMBIFORMES
Compact birds with rounded wings, short bills, and short legs and necks, such as doves and pigeons

ORDER: CORACIIFORMES
Compact birds with long bills and joined toes, such as kingfishers

ORDER: FALCONIFORMES
Birds of prey that hunt during the day, such as hawks, eagles, and vultures

ORDER: GALLIFORMES
Birds with rounded bodies, short wings, and well-developed legs that allow them to walk more than fly, such as fowl, turkeys, and quail

ORDER: PICIFORMES
Birds, such as woodpeckers and toucans, that usually have two back-facing toes instead of just one, making it easy for them to climb tree trunks

ORDER: STRIGIFORMES
Owls

ORDER: PASSERIFORMES
Birds that perch in trees, such as swallows, wrens, mockingbirds, robins, warblers, crows, cardinals, and sparrows

In the class Amphibia, there are only three orders. The best known are these two:

ORDER: CAUDATA
Long-tailed amphibians, such as salamanders and newts

ORDER: ANURA
Frogs, including toads

In the Reptilia class, the best known orders are these:

ORDER: TESTUDINES
Turtles

ORDER: SQUAMATA
Lizards and snakes

ORDER: CROCODILIA
Crocodiles, alligators, gharials, and caimans

There are too many orders in the Osteichthyes class to list here, but the most common order is:

ORDER: PERCIFORMES
Most fish species

There are also too many orders in the Insecta class to list here, but some of the more common ones are:

ORDER: LEPIDOPTERA
Butterflies and moths

ORDER: COLEOPTERA
Beetles

ORDER: ORTHOPTERA
Grasshoppers and crickets

ORDER: ODONATA
Dragonflies

ORDER: HYMENOPTERA
Ants, bees, and wasps

ORDER: DIPTERA
Flies

ORDER: PHASMATODEA
Walking sticks

In the class Malacostraca you will find many collectibles for your collections in the order Decapods. These include crayfish, crabs, and shrimp.

In the class Arachnida the two most likely orders you'll come across for your collection are spiders and scorpions.

FAMILY

After we've narrowed down what order an animal belongs to, the next classification below that is **family**. By now you'll have noticed that, as each grouping is split into smaller groups, the organisms within them are more and more alike. This is true at all levels, theoretically. So, for instance, rats and squirrels are in the same order, Rodentia—meaning they're both rodents—but they belong to their own families. Rats belong to the family Muridae. Squirrels belong to the family Sciuridae.

GENUS

Within families of animals, we can further classify them into a **genus**. A genus is a grouping that includes animals that have similar structures because they are genetically closely related. However, animals in a genus are not so similar that they can reproduce across groupings. For animals to be able to reproduce, they theoretically have to belong to the same species. So, for instance, in the rodent family Muridae, there is the genus *Rattus*, or rats, and the genus *Mus*, or mice. They're like cousins in the same family: related genetically, but not really the same.

SPECIES

A **species** consists of all the animals that are the same genetic type. They're able to breed and have offspring. For instance, rats are a genus of the family Muridae, but within that genus there are many species: Norway rats (*Rattus norvegicus*), black rats (*Rattus rattus*), pacific rats (*Rattus exulans*), etc. Each of these species have their own specific variations in color and size and even habits.

PART TWO

ANIM

{THE ANIMAL KINGDOM}

ALIA

Chordates • Arthropods • Mollusks •
Echinodermata, Cnidaria, and Porifera

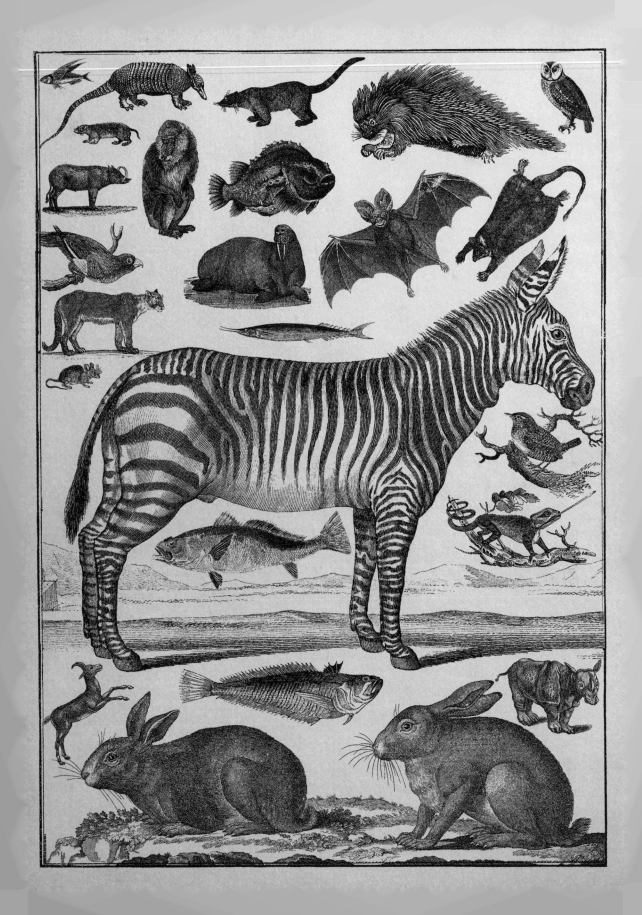

CHAPTER TWO

PHYLUM
CHORDATA

We've already said that all chordates have a long notochord—a stiff, hollow rod of cartilage running down their backs. To count as a chordate, an animal only has to have a notochord at some stage of its development. For example, many chordates only possess a notochord when they are embryos. In vertebrates such as mammals and birds, the notochord develops into a spine made of bones. In fact, several key traits of chordates may occur only in the embryos of some animals. Take the tail, for example. All chordates have tails, but some, like humans, don't retain the tail past the embryonic stage. We also don't retain the endostyle, a grooved passage in the throat that primitive chordates use to send food toward their stomachs. (In vertebrates, the endostyle probably develops into the thyroid, a gland below the Adam's apple that regulates

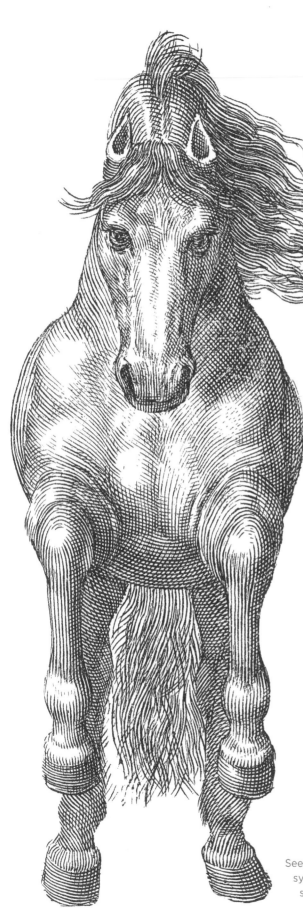

important chemical processes in the body.) Yet another trait we lose before birth is a set of pharyngeal slits, or openings in the throat. Primitive chordates, like the aquatic animals called tunicates, use these for sucking food from the water. One trait all chordates keep throughout life is bilateral symmetry. That means their bodies have a right and a left half which are mirror images of each other. For contrast, think of a starfish with five arms; it has no obvious right or left half.

Seen from the front, this horse is a good example of bilateral symmetry—a common trait among all chordates. Bilateral symmetry is when the right and left sides are the same.

MAMMALIA
(MAMMALS)

THE WORD MAMMAL IS MODERN, FROM THE SCIENTIFIC NAME MAMMALIA COINED BY CARL LINNAEUS IN 1758, DERIVED FROM THE LATIN MAMMA (MEANING "TEAT" OR "PAP").

Along with birds, reptiles, amphibians, and most fish, mammals are a class of animals in the phylum of chordates. They have several features that distinguish them from the other classes of animals: They have hair or fur, a lower jaw that consists of a single bone, and three bones inside their middle ear. The females also have mammary glands, which allow them to nurse their young.

There are more than five thousand species of mammals. These include the egg-laying monotremes (platypuses and echidnas); marsupials, which keep their young in a pouch for a while after birth (kangaroos, koalas, wombats, and others); and placentals, which give birth to live young and don't keep them in pouches. That last group includes rabbits, rodents, cats, dogs, elephants, deer, donkeys, horses, cattle, bats, pigs, and many other familiar animals.

Placentals such as bears give birth to live young and don't keep them in pouches.

Marsupials such as kangaroos keep their young in a pouch after birth.

Monotremes such as platypuses lay eggs.

SKULLS AND TEETH

A skull is the bony bowl that protects an animal's brain. Not all animals have skulls. For example, insects and octopuses don't have any bones at all. But mammals do—and their skulls and teeth can be pretty easy to find for a budding collector.

In most mammals, the upper teeth are attached to the skull. The bottom teeth are attached to the lower jaw. The lower jaw is not part of the skull. When the animal is alive, the lower jaw is attached to the skull by soft tissues. After an animal dies, those soft tissues decay. So if you find a skull in the wild, you may not find the lower jaw with it. Both pieces—the lower jaw and the skull—are fun to collect. Often, the teeth will remain planted in the skull or lower jaw, which can help you figure out what kind of a skull you have. Each mammal has a certain number of each kind of tooth. Scientists call this information a "dental formula." It is the first thing they look at when they want to identify a skull.

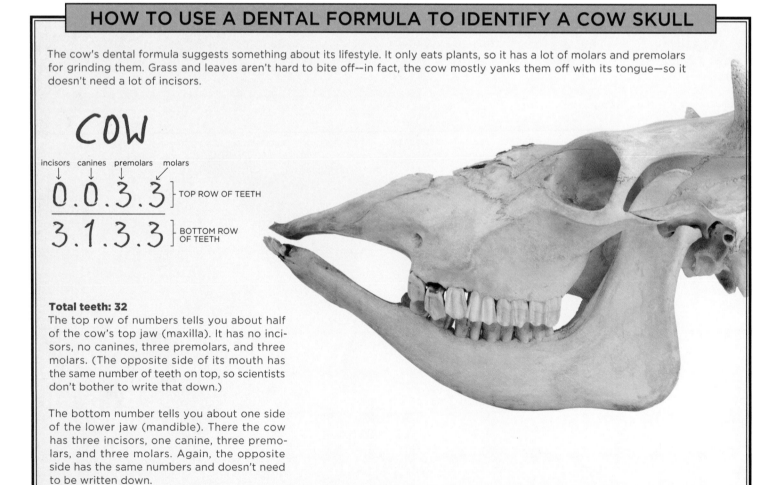

HOW TO USE A DENTAL FORMULA TO IDENTIFY A COW SKULL

The cow's dental formula suggests something about its lifestyle. It only eats plants, so it has a lot of molars and premolars for grinding them. Grass and leaves aren't hard to bite off—in fact, the cow mostly yanks them off with its tongue—so it doesn't need a lot of incisors.

COW

incisors · canines · premolars · molars

0 . 0 . 3 . 3] TOP ROW OF TEETH
_____
3 . 1 . 3 . 3] BOTTOM ROW OF TEETH

Total teeth: 32
The top row of numbers tells you about half of the cow's top jaw (maxilla). It has no incisors, no canines, three premolars, and three molars. (The opposite side of its mouth has the same number of teeth on top, so scientists don't bother to write that down.)

The bottom number tells you about one side of the lower jaw (mandible). There the cow has three incisors, one canine, three premolars, and three molars. Again, the opposite side has the same numbers and doesn't need to be written down.

CAT

$$\frac{3.1.3.1}{3.1.2.1}$$

Total teeth: 30
Cats don't usually eat plants, so they have few molars. Their molars and hind premolars form special meat-shearing teeth called carnassials.

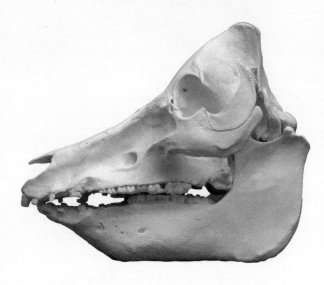

PIG

$$\frac{3.1.4.3}{3.1.4.3}$$

Total teeth: 44
Can you guess what pigs eat? Actually, they eat almost everything, including plants and animals. Since they're omnivores, they need plenty of strong teeth in every position.

RACCOON

$$\frac{3.1.4.2}{3.1.4.2}$$

Total teeth: 40
Raccoons are omnivores, equipped with a variety of teeth suited for meat or plants.

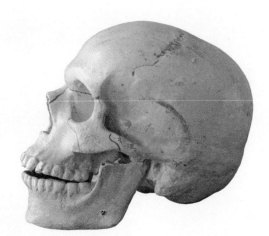

HUMAN

$$\frac{2.1.2.3}{2.1.2.3}$$

Total teeth: 32
Adults have this many teeth, assuming they haven't lost any to accidents or tooth decay. Kids first grow a deciduous, or temporary, set of teeth. As these fall out, they are replaced by the permanent set. Some people never grow the back set of molars, or wisdom teeth, so they have only 28.

A SKULL WILL OFTEN TURN YELLOW AS IT DRIES OUT, SO A GOOD WAY TO PRESERVE IT IS TO PAINT IT WHITE. NOT ONLY DOES THE PAINT KEEP IT FROM TURNING YELLOW (AND DRYING OUT AND BREAKING), IT ALSO FILLS IN THE LITTLE HOLES. ACRYLIC ENAMEL PAINT IS A GOOD CHOICE.

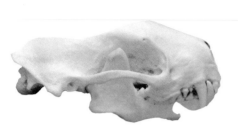

Skunk (genus *Mephitis*)

DOMAIN: EUKARYOTA
KINGDOM: ANIMALIA
PHYLUM: CHORDATA
CLASS: MAMMALIA
ORDER: CARNIVORA
FAMILY: MEPHITIDAE
GENUS: *Mephitis*

There are twelve different species of skunks. Skunks eat a wide variety of foods including insects, worms, plants, garbage, and pet food people leave out for their cats and dogs. That last habit often brings them into conflict with humans. The skunk usually wins. Unlike many wild animals, skunks don't readily run away when confronted by a human. Their ability to spray a horrible-smelling fluid makes them bold. They keep eating what they want and only waddle away when they're done.

Like most carnivoras, they also eat meat. They obtain the meat by preying on small animals like lizards, frogs, and mice, and also by scavenging—eating animals that are already dead. Their skulls match their meat-eating ways. The dental formula of one common species, the striped skunk (*Mephitis mephitis*), is $\frac{3.1.3.1}{3.1.3.2}$. The skull is small enough to hold in your palm, and the ridge of carnassial teeth will be clearly visible on the sides. Other teeth often fall out after death, but in a good specimen you'll still be able to see the holes they were in.

WHERE TO FIND Almost all the species of skunks can be found in the Americas. The striped skunk, which is the most common one, can be found throughout North America. Skunks favor open lands next to forested areas, but can adapt to a variety of habitats, and it is not uncommon for them to burrow under porches or homes.

Goat (genus *Capra*)

DOMAIN: EUKARYOTA
KINGDOM: ANIMALIA
PHYLUM: CHORDATA
CLASS: MAMMALIA
ORDER: ARTIODACTYLA
FAMILY: BOVIDAE
GENUS: *Capra*

The goat has been closely associated with humans for at least ten thousand years, and it's become one of the most useful animals. Its milk is suitable for drinking. (It tastes stronger and less sweet than cow's milk.) Its meat is a staple in some parts of the world. Its hide can be made into clothes. Even the hair of some breeds can be spun into wool.

Goat skulls are a common item for a collection because they are fairly easy to find. Goats can be found in the wild or on farms. Many of them have two long, curved horns protruding from the top of their skulls. The dental formula is $\frac{0.0.3.3}{3.1.3.3}$. If you find the skull without the lower jaw, there will be no teeth at all in front, only the flattened premolars and molars in back. That's because a goat mostly eats plants.

WHERE TO FIND Goats, both domesticated and wild, can be found nearly everywhere in the world.

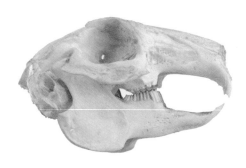

Squirrel (genus *Sciurus*)

DOMAIN: EUKARYOTA
KINGDOM: ANIMALIA
PHYLUM: CHORDATA
CLASS: MAMMALIA
ORDER: RODENTIA
FAMILY: SCIURIDAE
GENUS: *Sciurus*

Squirrel skulls are small enough to fit in the palm of your hand. Squirrels, like other rodents, have unusual teeth. At the very front of a squirrel's head are a few very long, sharp incisors. The squirrel's incisors can bite off a chunk of food, like ours do, but they are also good at gnawing on things, like the hard shells of nuts. The squirrel wears its incisors down gnawing through hard things, but they grow fast to keep up with the wear. (Rats, which are also rodents, can even gnaw through concrete and steel.)

Rodents—including squirrels, rats, mice, gerbils, guinea pigs, beavers, and others—lack canine teeth. Where their canine teeth would be, there's an empty space. The rodent uses this empty space for holding on to things it wants to gnaw—like acorns. With an acorn held tight in that empty jaw space, a squirrel can really get to work with its incisors. In the case of one common species called the Eastern gray squirrel (*Sciurus carolinensis*), the empty space is big enough for a walnut. The squirrel's molars—typically three on each side of the top jaw—are tiny compared to a person's.

Another prominent feature of a squirrel skull is the big eye holes, or eye sockets. For a small animal, a squirrel has enormous eyes. It uses them to look around for predators. Squirrels need excellent vision to help them judge leaps between branches.

WHERE TO FIND Squirrels can be found throughout North America, South America, Europe, and Asia.

Cow (genus *Bos*)

DOMAIN: EUKARYOTA
KINGDOM: ANIMALIA
PHYLUM: CHORDATA
CLASS: MAMMALIA
ORDER: ARTIODACTYLA
FAMILY: BOVIDAE
GENUS: *Bos*

At first glance, a cow's skull doesn't look like it came from a cow. It lacks the broad, velvety nose and the twitchy ears. These parts are made of soft tissue rather than bone, so they don't last. There's nothing left of its ears to let you know what powerful instruments they were. A cow can hear sounds too deep and too high for human ears.

The nose is another matter. Even though the fleshy end is gone, the skull will still reveal the long snout. The large size of the snout is a hint that the cow also had a good sense of smell. Cattle can sometimes detect predators miles away just by scent.

Then there are the eyes. Their sockets are placed on the sides of the head so that the cow can see in almost every direction at once. This is a useful trait for a prey species that must constantly watch for predators.

WHERE TO FIND There are over a billion cows in the world, making them one of the most plentiful mammals on the planet. They can be found on every continent.

ANTLERS

Antlers are pointed, bony structures that deer grow on their heads. In most species, only the males grow antlers. An exception is the reindeer, or caribou (*Rangifer tarandus*). Both male and female reindeer have antlers.

Antlers can be different shapes, depending on the species. For example, a moose (*Alces alces*) has "palmate" antlers, which means each of its antlers looks like a hand, with a flat part and then some fingerlike points. The antlers of a white-tailed deer (*Odocoileus virginianus*) look more like tree branches, with no flat part.

Male deer use their antlers to fight each other. They do that to impress females. The bigger their antlers, the better they do in fights, and the better their chances of mating. The male starts growing his antlers in the spring. As the antlers grow, they are covered with a soft kind of skin called velvet, which dries up after they are fully grown. The male scrapes the velvet off by rubbing his head against trees and bushes. Mating time happens in the fall, after which the males shed their antlers.

WHITE-TAILED DEER SHED THEIR ANTLERS IN THE FALL AND EARLY WINTER. ELK RETAIN THEIR ANTLERS THROUGH MARCH. BE CAREFUL WHERE YOU COLLECT ANTLERS FROM. IT IS ILLEGAL TO COLLECT ANTLERS IN NATIONAL PARKS, FOR INSTANCE, BECAUSE SHED ANTLERS ARE CONSIDERED PART OF A PARK'S ECOSYSTEM. SHED ANTLERS PROVIDE CALCIUM TO SMALL MAMMALS THAT GNAW ON THEM.

WHERE TO FIND Sometimes you can find these shed antlers lying around in woods. They look and feel like wood. Shed antlers are not very heavy. If you keep them dry and indoors, they don't need to be preserved. They will last just the way they are.

HORNS

Many different animals have horns. Mostly, horns are made of bone on the inside, surrounded by a tough material similar to fingernails called keratin. They come in all shapes and sizes. Most animals with horns don't shed them. Sometimes horns are used exactly like antlers—to impress females and battle other males. Sometimes they're for defense against predators. For example, the sable antelope (*Hippotragus niger*) has been known to kill lions with its horns.

WHERE TO FIND The horns of cattle are pretty easy to find. Farmers and ranchers often cut the horns off so their cattle won't hurt anybody with them. At the wide end, a cattle horn is about as big around as a baseball.

TYPES OF ANTLERS AND HORNS

Antlers and *horns* are sometimes used interchangeably, but they're actually very different features on animal skulls.

The antlers of the white-tailed deer (*Odocoileus virginianus*) look like tree branches.

Bull (*Bos taurus*) horns can vary greatly in shape, dependent on species.

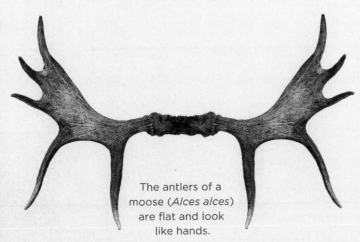

The antlers of a moose (*Alces alces*) are flat and look like hands.

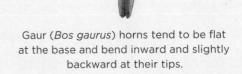

Gaur (*Bos gaurus*) horns tend to be flat at the base and bend inward and slightly backward at their tips.

The antlers of the elk (*Cervus canadensis*) branch out like those of the white-tailed deer and reindeer, but they are not covered in velvet.

Water buffalo (*Bubalus bubalis*) horns grow outward in a semicircle, but remain on the plane of the forehead.

CLAWS

Most mammals and birds, and some reptiles, have claws on their toes. These are made of the protein keratin. Humans, of course, have fingernails and toenails, but we don't call these claws because they don't come to sharp points. Some mammals, like horses and cows, have thick, strong nails that cover their toes completely. These are called hooves. But animals like skunks, raccoons, cats, dogs, hyenas, bats, rats, and bears have true claws.

Canada Lynx (*Lynx canadensis*)

DOMAIN: EUKARYOTA
KINGDOM: ANIMALIA
PHYLUM: CHORDATA
CLASS: MAMMALIA
ORDER: CARNIVORA
FAMILY: FELIDAE
GENUS: *Lynx*
SPECIES: *L. canadensis*

A lynx is a catlike animal with tufts of hair sticking up from its ears. Its feet are very wide so it can walk well on snow. Its tail is short and stubby. It's about twice the size of a house cat. The claws of a lynx are about an inch long. They are usually gray with some red or brown on them and much more curved than other animal's claws. They are thinner and sharper, too.

WHERE TO FIND The Canada lynx can be found across most of Canada and Alaska, and in some forested areas in the northern US.

CATS PREVENT THEIR CLAWS FROM GETTING WORN DOWN BY KEEPING THEM OUT OF THE WAY WHILE THEY WALK. THEY BRING THEIR CLAWS OUT WHEN THEY NEED THEM—FOR EXAMPLE, WHEN THEY WANT TO CLIMB A TREE, OR HUNT.

North American Black Bear
(*Ursus americanus*)

DOMAIN: EUKARYOTA
KINGDOM: ANIMALIA
PHYLUM: CHORDATA
CLASS: MAMMALIA
ORDER: CARNIVORA
FAMILY: URSIDAE
GENUS: *Ursus*
SPECIES: *U. americanus*

The North American black bear has a slightly confusing name. Most black bears are black, but some are brown, cinnamon-colored, or even a light blue gray. They are omnivores, eating plant matter like berries and roots as well as animals like fish, young deer, and insects. They love honey, too. Their claws are shaped like broken half-moons. The bear uses them to dig for roots and insects and to climb trees.

WHERE TO FIND Black bears are native to North America and can usually be found in forested areas.

Gray Wolf (*Canis lupus*)

DOMAIN: EUKARYOTA
KINGDOM: ANIMALIA
PHYLUM: CHORDATA
CLASS: MAMMALIA
ORDER: CARNIVORA
FAMILY: CANIDAE
GENUS: *Canis*
SPECIES: *C. lupus*

Gray wolves are predators that live in a complex social structure. By hunting in packs, they can kill even huge hoofed mammals such as moose. Dogs are a domesticated form of the gray wolf. Their claws are used to attack their prey and provide traction, allowing them a better grip on slippery surfaces.

WHERE TO FIND Gray wolves can be found throughout North America, Europe, Asia, and Africa. They can adapt to cold weather, deserts, grasslands, and are usually found in forested areas.

Coyote (*Canis latrans*)

DOMAIN: EUKARYOTA
KINGDOM: ANIMALIA
PHYLUM: CHORDATA
CLASS: MAMMALIA
ORDER: CARNIVORA
FAMILY: CANIDAE
GENUS: *Canis*
SPECIES: *C. latrans*

Coyotes are related to wolves and dogs. They live in many parts of the US. Sometimes they even live in big cities like New York, Los Angeles, and Chicago. Their claws are usually smooth, black, and thick. They are about an inch long and only slightly curved.

WHERE TO FIND Coyotes are native to North America, and can be found as far south as Central America and as far north as Alaska.

HOW TO IDENTIFY ANIMAL TRACKS IN THE WILD

Every mammal leaves a different kind of track. Partly, that's because they all have different claws or nails. Here are some tricks that will help you figure out what kind of animal left a track. You can start with a very basic identifier: Does the track seem to have one, two, three, four or five "fingers"? If it's anything but three, you're probably looking at a mammal. Birds' tracks tend to have three fingers. Also, is there a line between the footprints? That's the drag mark of a tail, which would immediately rule out short-tailed animals like rabbits or bobcats.

Do the tracks alternate? When animals are walking, one foot moves forward at a time. When animals hop, the two back feet stay together. So if you're looking at two footprints next to each other, it's a good bet you're looking at an animal that hops, like a rabbit.

Do the footprints have hard edges? Hard-edged shapes are usually made by hoofed animals like horses or cattle. Some animals, like horses, walk only on their middle toes. You can't really even see their other toes. Other hooved animals, like deer, walk on two toes. Their tracks look like paired half-moons. Each hoofed animal—pigs, cattle, sheep, and so on—has a somewhat different hoof shape.

Does the footprint look like a little handprint? It's probably a raccoon's. Raccoons dunk their food in water. This curious behavior, known as "dabbling," probably helps them sort out their food with their sensitive fingers.

Are the tracks large and like blunt, fat human feet? Watch out, that's a bear track. A bear track will have little points where its claws dug into the ground, so you probably won't confuse them with human tracks. Humans and bears are unusual: We put our heels on the ground when we walk. In most mammals, the heel is higher up so it doesn't hit the ground. It appears as another bend in the leg.

Is the track soft-edged and trapezoidal? Members of the dog and cat families leave pad marks. Their tracks have a trapezoidal shape, and you'll see the toe prints as separate dots. Dog prints will have claw marks; cat prints won't.

Are they missing claw marks? Since cats can retract their claws, there are no claw marks in a cat footprint. A domestic cat's footprint will be about 1½".

How wide is the footprint? A bobcat's footprint will be anywhere between 2" and 3", and a mountain lion's might be almost 5" wide!

Skunk tracks show five toes, with the longer claws showing on the front feet. Why do skunks have longer claws on their front feet? They use their front paws to dig up roots, which is where they find insects to eat.

Human feet are easy to distinguish, though it's not common to see bare feet in the wild!

QUILLS

The only mammals that have quills are porcupines. People sometimes confuse hedgehogs with porcupines, but, in fact, they aren't even in the same order of mammals. Hedgehogs are more closely related to shrews and moles than they are to porcupines. They have stiff, hollow hairs called spines, which are often confused with quills. Unlike the quills of a porcupine, a hedgehog's spines cannot be easily removed.

Porcupine (family Erethizontidae)

DOMAIN: EUKARYOTA
KINGDOM: ANIMALIA
PHYLUM: CHORDATA
CLASS: MAMMALIA
ORDER: RODENTIA
FAMILY: ERETHIZONTIDAE

A porcupine is a kind of rodent. It is covered in quills, which are hard and sharp. These quills are really just hairs that are covered in thick plates of keratin, which is the material found in fingernails. When a predator attacks, the porcupine sticks these quills straight up in the air. The predator bites and gets stabbed. The quills stick in the predator's mouth and nose. Usually, that makes the predator go away. Sometimes dogs attack porcupines and end up with more than one hundred quills in their faces. When a quill sticks into a predator's flesh, its tip breaks apart. That makes it very hard to pull out.

The quills can be a serious problem. Sometimes a predator can't get them out, and the wounds get infected. Even big, powerful predators like tigers can die from the infected wounds. Some porcupines don't wait to get bitten. They stick up their quills and run backward toward a predator, trying to stick him.

In North America, porcupines usually have quills 3 inches long or less. They are usually white with black tips. Other porcupines from Africa have much bigger quills. They can grow to more than 10 inches long.

WHERE TO FIND New World porcupines probably originated in South America and migrated north. Now they are found in wooded regions across North America, Central America, and northern regions of South America. Old World porcupines are found all over southern Europe, Africa, India, and parts of Southeast Asia.

PORCUPINES ARE NOT DANGEROUS TO PEOPLE, UNLESS THE PEOPLE TRY TO PICK THEM UP.

AVES
(BIRDS)

From parakeets to penguins, from ostriches to owls, all birds have feathers. The only other animals that had feathers were certain small, fast-running dinosaurs. In fact, birds evolved from this suborder of dinosaurs, which are known as theropods. Their closest relatives among animals living now are crocodiles and alligators, which are also descended from this group.

All birds lay eggs with hard shells (see page 56). Most birds take care of their young, feeding them long after they have hatched. There are about ten thousand species of birds. They can be found everywhere in the world and are known to migrate great distances. They range in size from the tiny hummingbird, which is 2 inches long, to the ostrich, which is 9 feet tall.

All birds have beaks, which are made out of keratin, the same protein that makes claws and hooves and nails and horns and quills. The bird uses its beak to gather or hunt for food, to build nests, and to feed its young.

All birds have wings, although not all birds fly with those wings. When a bird breathes, much of the air flows past its lungs and directly into cavities inside its bones. These hollow bones then fill with air, which helps to enable flight.

Like most mammals, birds are warm-blooded.

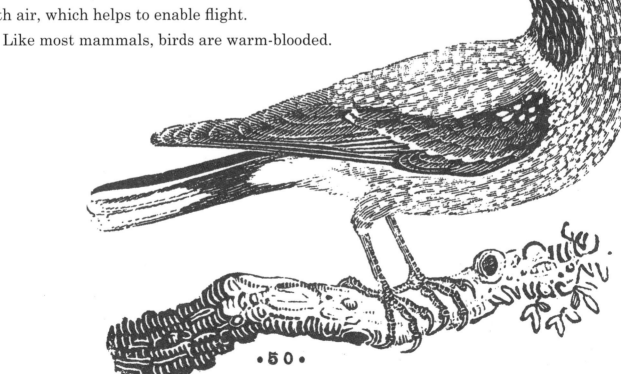

FEATHERS

Feathers have a lot of jobs. First of all, they can help a bird stay warm. Second, they can help a bird fly. Of course, not all birds fly. But even in flightless birds, the feathers still help the bird move. For example, ostriches use the fluffy feathers on their wings to help them steer as they run. A third use for feathers is waterproofing. Water runs off the feathers of most birds without getting their skin wet. A fourth job for feathers is color. Birds use color in lots of ways. For example, it helps some birds find others of their species. In many species, bright color is a way for the males to attract females. Color is what makes feathers especially interesting for a collector.

Birds have several kinds of feathers. Most of the ones you see are vaned feathers. A vaned feather has a stem called a rachis running up the middle. The rachis is made of a material similar to horns or claws, but it is much tougher. Usually it will bend, but it is very tough to tear or break. Little branches come out of the rachis, usually in neat rows. These branches are called barbs. Barbs can be soft as hairs or very stiff.

Feathers have different functions, so they come in different shapes and sizes. These are the most common types of feathers we might find.

Wing feathers are made for flight. One side is wider than the other to literally cut through the air when flying. Since wing feathers support the bird during flight, they are the strongest and largest of all the bird's feathers.

Tail feathers are symmetrical on both sides of the rachis. They provide stability and control while flying, as well as precision steering.

Semiplume feathers keep a bird warm. They're fluffy like down feathers, but they have a rachis. Semiplume feathers are short and soft, and are found underneath other feathers.

CROWS HAVE THE BIGGEST BRAINS IN PROPORTION TO THEIR BODIES OF ALL BIRD SPECIES.
THEIR "CAWING" IS ACTUALLY A COMPLEX FORM OF LANGUAGE THAT HAS DIFFERENT MEANINGS AT DIFFERENT TIMES.
THEY CAN MIMIC THE SOUNDS OF OTHER ANIMALS, INCLUDING THE HUMAN VOICE.

Crow (genus *Corvus*)

DOMAIN: EUKARYOTA
KINGDOM: ANIMALIA
PHYLUM: CHORDATA
CLASS: AVES
ORDER: PASSERIFORMES
FAMILY: CORVIDAE
GENUS: *Corvus*

The order Passeriformes is a huge group containing more than five thousand species, many of which look very different from each other. The family Corvidae includes crows, ravens, jays, and magpies, among others.

Many crows are shiny and black. You may also see crows that have gray or white mixed in with the black. Up close, the black feathers sometimes look more like a dark, dusty brown.

Crows are very smart birds. Some of them have learned to say words. Other have been seen using pieces of grass to fish bugs out of a hole. Such use of tools is considered a sign of intelligence in an animal. Scientists from Oxford University conducted an experiment to test how smart crows are about using tools. They put some food at the bottom of a can and offered a pair of crows two tools to fish it out with—a hooked wire and a straight wire. The first crow chose the hook and went to work. That proved the crow was smart enough to figure out which tool to use and how to use it. The second crow surprised the scientists. She bent the straight wire into a hook and went to work beside her partner. Not only was she smart enough to use a tool, she was also smart enough to make a tool.

Crows are easy to find. They live almost everywhere. Some birds fly to warmer places for the winter. Crows don't. You can watch them all year round.

You can also feed crows. To do that, you can find or build a feeding platform. A feeding platform is a flat place that is easy for birds to get to. It should be hard for cats and other animals to reach. Crows don't like to eat at a place where a cat might attack them or take their feed. You can use the roof of a shed or a garage as a feeder, or you can build one by nailing a wooden platform into a tree. Then, put your table scraps on the feeder. If you leave food regularly, crows will find it and learn to look for it there. They will eat meat scraps, apple peels and cores, bread, nuts, fruits, and vegetables. They will pick meat from chicken or turkey bones; they will pick bits of corn from a cob. They will even eat road-killed animals.

In fact, crows are famous for eating dead animals they find on the road or beach. They have been seen eating snakes, raccoons, cats, rabbits, deer, pigeons, seagulls, bony fish, sharks, cattle, and seals. They aren't always strong enough to break through the skin of a big animal such as a deer, so they may wait for bigger scavengers, like wolves, coyotes, badgers, or eagles to tear through the hide first.

But what if there's no big scavenger around to help? Sometimes the crows find an eagle and lead it back to the dead animal. At other times these birds are enemies, but in this situation they help each other.

WHERE TO FIND Crows are found on every continent except South America. They live in cities and urban areas, as well as rural and countryside regions.

Peacock (genus *Pavo*)

DOMAIN: EUKARYOTA
KINGDOM: ANIMALIA
PHYLUM: CHORDATA
CLASS: AVES
ORDER: GALLIFORMES
FAMILY: PHASIANIDAE
GENUS: *Pavo*

This animal is really called a peafowl. It belongs to the order Galliformes, which includes the heavy birds that feed mostly on the ground, like turkeys and grouse. The peafowl is in the family Phasianidae, which includes pheasants, quail, and chickens.

Only the males are called peacocks; the females are peahens. Peafowl show sexual dimorphism. That means the males and the females look very different. The females are brown or gray and about the size of a chicken; they look pretty dull compared to the males, which are quite impressive looking. For example, a male might have blue feathers on his body that seem dark and shiny at the same time; on his head, little feathers that look like a goofy haircut; and on his rear end, speckled brown-and-white, orange, gold, and white feathers. But the ones everybody notices are the feathers on the tail, which are long and turquoise with lovely, fluffy barbs.

A peacock can make these turquoise feathers stand up and spread out. This may make him as tall as a man and a yard wide. On the feathers are spots of blue, brown, and green that look like huge eyes.

WHERE TO FIND Originally from South Asia, the peacock was introduced and thrives in many other parts of the world, including North and South America, South Africa, and Australia.

Pigeon (*Columba livia*)

DOMAIN: EUKARYOTA
KINGDOM: ANIMALIA
PHYLUM: CHORDATA
CLASS: AVES
ORDER: COLUMBIFORMES
FAMILY: COLUMBIDAE
GENUS: *Columba*
SPECIES: *C. livia*

Pigeons are among the oldest human companions. They may first have been domesticated ten thousand years ago. The species still exists in the wild—it's known as the rock dove, and it specializes in living on the ledges of cliffs. It's one of the few species that has benefitted from the development of cities. Pigeons treat city buildings as cliffs and nest on their ledges. A wild rock dove is usually grayish-blue, with two black bars on its wings. Its head may be blue, green, or gray. Feathers from such birds show some combination of those colors. Here's where domestication adds an interesting wrinkle, though. People have used selective breeding to develop pigeons of many different colors, from rust-red to speckled brown to pure black or pure white. Some even have magenta feathers on the breast. Since wild pigeons and tame ones interbreed, all of these colors can now be found in the wild. You could build a collection with dozens of different feathers just from pigeons.

WHERE TO FIND Pigeons can be found everywhere in the world: cities, urban areas, farmland, cliffs, and rocky promontories.

Ostrich (*Struthio camelus*)

DOMAIN: EUKARYOTA
KINGDOM: ANIMALIA
PHYLUM: CHORDATA
CLASS: AVES
ORDER: STRUTHIONIFORMES
FAMILY: STRUTHIONIDAE
GENUS: *Struthio*
SPECIES: *S. camelus*

The order Struthioniformes includes mostly flightless, fast-running birds such as emus, rheas, cassowaries, and kiwis. The Struthionidae family, however, only includes ostriches and their extinct prehistoric relatives.

Ostriches are the biggest birds on earth. Some grow to more than 9 feet tall. Their eyes are about 2 inches across—much bigger than a person's eyes.

Because they are such big animals, ostrich feathers are very large, often reaching more than one foot long. The feathers can be black, white, gray, or pale brown, and are very fluffy. The ostrich uses them to shade its eggs. The feather dusters people use to clean their houses are often made of ostrich feathers.

WHERE TO FIND Ostriches are native to Africa.

Rooster (*Gallus gallus*)

DOMAIN: EUKARYOTA
KINGDOM: ANIMALIA
PHYLUM: CHORDATA
CLASS: AVES
ORDER: GALLIFORMES
FAMILY: PHASIANIDAE
GENUS: *Gallus*
SPECIES: *G. gallus*

The chicken is a domesticated form of the red jungle fowl. Wild or tame, chickens can live on what they scratch up from the dirt—seeds, worms, and insects, for example. They are surprisingly tough predators and will occasionally eat mice, lizards, and even rattlesnakes.

The wild male red jungle fowl (the rooster) is spectacular. Different parts of its body are covered with not just red feathers, but also orange, black, blue, brown, gray, and turquoise ones. The wild female (the hen) is less colorful, but still shows interesting patterns of brown and orange.

Like the pigeon, the domestic chicken has been selectively bred into many different colors and body types. Some breeds produce a lot of eggs. Some grow a lot of meat. Some breeds are even selected for sport fighting, though this practice is now illegal in many places. Like their wild relatives, the rooster tends to be more colorful than the hen. He also typically has longer feathers on his neck and tail. But both genders can produce attractive feathers. Specialists recognize more than sixty breeds, and many of those have variants, yielding hundreds of color combinations. For example, the Java breed is black with white spots that look like big drops of snow. The Polish breed has dozens of variants, including one with elegant beige feathers trimmed in white. Some of those feathers surround its face like the mane of a lion. The Rhode Island Red breed can vary from light orange to a dark brown with red highlights.

WHERE TO FIND Chickens and roosters are found on farms around the world.

TYPES OF FEATHERS

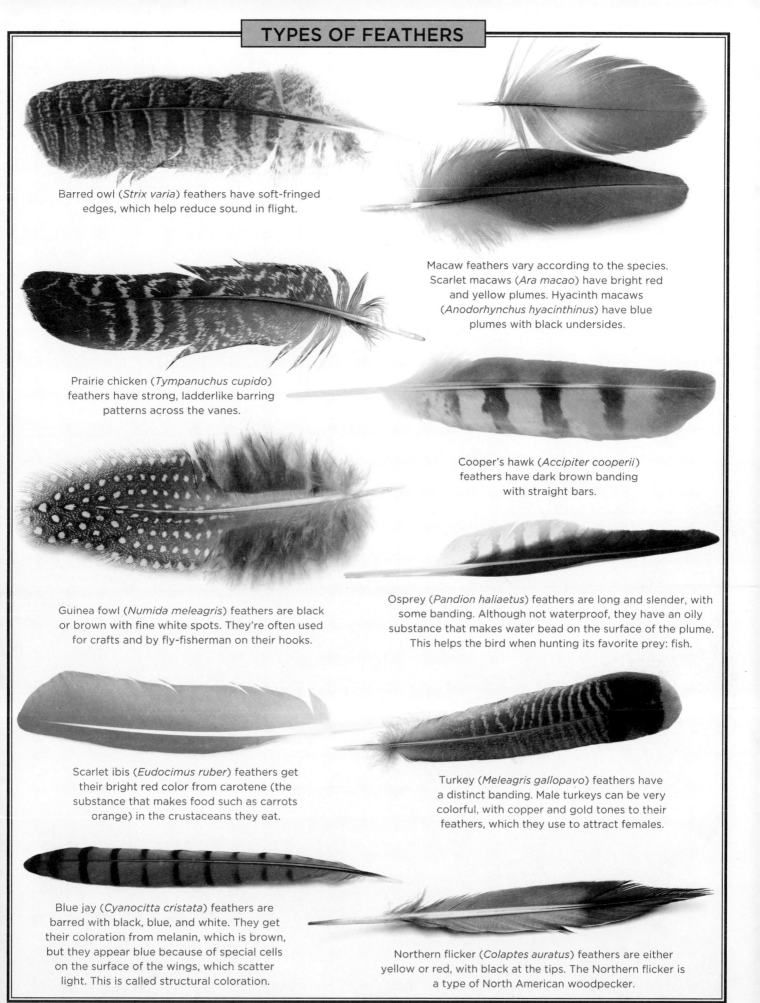

Barred owl (*Strix varia*) feathers have soft-fringed edges, which help reduce sound in flight.

Macaw feathers vary according to the species. Scarlet macaws (*Ara macao*) have bright red and yellow plumes. Hyacinth macaws (*Anodorhynchus hyacinthinus*) have blue plumes with black undersides.

Prairie chicken (*Tympanuchus cupido*) feathers have strong, ladderlike barring patterns across the vanes.

Cooper's hawk (*Accipiter cooperii*) feathers have dark brown banding with straight bars.

Guinea fowl (*Numida meleagris*) feathers are black or brown with fine white spots. They're often used for crafts and by fly-fisherman on their hooks.

Osprey (*Pandion haliaetus*) feathers are long and slender, with some banding. Although not waterproof, they have an oily substance that makes water bead on the surface of the plume. This helps the bird when hunting its favorite prey: fish.

Scarlet ibis (*Eudocimus ruber*) feathers get their bright red color from carotene (the substance that makes food such as carrots orange) in the crustaceans they eat.

Turkey (*Meleagris gallopavo*) feathers have a distinct banding. Male turkeys can be very colorful, with copper and gold tones to their feathers, which they use to attract females.

Blue jay (*Cyanocitta cristata*) feathers are barred with black, blue, and white. They get their coloration from melanin, which is brown, but they appear blue because of special cells on the surface of the wings, which scatter light. This is called structural coloration.

Northern flicker (*Colaptes auratus*) feathers are either yellow or red, with black at the tips. The Northern flicker is a type of North American woodpecker.

EGGS

Birds, as everybody knows, lay eggs with hard shells. This is unusual. Animals like frogs lay eggs with no shell at all. They are held in a kind of jelly. Many snakes lay eggs with soft, leathery shells. Only a few animals other than birds, such as certain turtles and insects, lay hard-shelled eggs. Hard shells help protect the eggs from getting smashed, drying out, or getting infected with germs. Bird shells also contain calcium. Calcium is a mineral that young birds need for growth, so the shell is a source of nutrition.

For many birds, the primary color of their eggs is white. Many perching birds, however, produce colored eggs. Since eggs are a primary source of nourishment for many animals, some ground-nesting birds produce eggs that are well camouflaged in their surrounding environment. The color comes from pigments that are added to the shell while it is still inside the mother.

Despite appearances, the eggshell is actually not a solid structure. It has tiny holes in it called pores that allow gases, like oxygen, to pass through the egg.

Bird eggs mostly have the same oval shape, but they come in different sizes and colors. As you might expect, the biggest eggs come from the biggest birds. Ostrich eggs are the size of footballs!

> IF YOU WANT TO TRY COLLECTING EGGS IN THE WILD, BE SURE TO CHECK THE LOCAL LAWS AND MAKE SURE IT'S OKAY. (YOU CAN DO THIS BY ASKING YOUR STATE'S WILDLIFE DEPARTMENT.) GENERALLY, YOU SHOULD ONLY COLLECT EGGS THAT WON'T HATCH ANYWAY—FOR EXAMPLE, EGGS THAT HAVE FALLEN OUT OF A NEST OR HAVE BEEN ABANDONED. IT'S UNWISE EVEN TO HANDLE EGGS FROM AN ACTIVE NEST; THE PARENT BIRDS MAY BE FRIGHTENED AWAY, CAUSING THE CHICKS TO DIE FROM LACK OF INCUBATION.

American Robin (*Turdus migratorius*)

DOMAIN: EUKARYOTA
KINGDOM: ANIMALIA
PHYLUM: CHORDATA
CLASS: AVES
ORDER: PASSERIFORMES
FAMILY: TURDIDAE
GENUS: *Turdus*
SPECIES: *T. migratorius*

The American robin is famous as a symbol of spring. It doesn't necessarily migrate for the winter, but it becomes more active and visible during the spring. It's easy to recognize because of its red or orange chest. Because it's one of the first birds of the year to brood (produce offspring), it may find no leafy trees to build a nest in. Instead, it builds its first nest of the year in an evergreen tree, such as a cedar. The female builds the nest on a flat branch or fork. She lays three to five eggs, which are usually pale blue or turquoise and a little more than an inch long. Sometimes there are dark speckles. She may lay up to three clutches, or broods, of eggs per year, each in a new nest.

WHERE TO FIND Robin nests are usually located in a fork of a tree or sometimes in a bush. Robins are also known to nest on building ledges. They can be found across North America. In the winter, many robins fly south to wooded areas that have berry-producing trees.

Blue Jay (*Cyanocitta cristata*)

DOMAIN: EUKARYOTA
KINGDOM: ANIMALIA
PHYLUM: CHORDATA
CLASS: AVES
ORDER: PASSERIFORMES
FAMILY: CORVIDAE
GENUS: *Cyanocitta*
SPECIES: *C. cristata*

The blue jay is patterned with black and white as well as blue. It has a crest of feathers on its head. A careful bird-watcher can tell individual jays apart by the black stripes on their faces and necks. Blue jays make a lot of noise, and they're expert mimics. They can imitate crows, hawks, and even dogs. Like their cousin the crow, they are intelligent. Captive jays have been known to get food inside their cages by dragging the paper the food was resting on.

A mother jay lays one clutch of eggs per year, containing two to seven eggs. They are slightly more than an inch long and usually light blue or light brown, and often thickly speckled.

WHERE TO FIND Native to North America, blue jays are found in most of eastern and central US and southeastern Canada. They nest in woods and forests, but also near residential communities.

Northern Mockingbird (*Mimus polyglottos*)

DOMAIN: EUKARYOTA
KINGDOM: ANIMALIA
PHYLUM: CHORDATA
CLASS: AVES
ORDER: PASSERIFORMES
FAMILY: MIMIDAE
GENUS: *Mimus*
SPECIES: *M. polyglottos*

The slender northern mockingbird is gray and white with bars of brown. It gets its name by imitating other birds; sometimes it will run through the songs of a dozen other kinds of birds in a row. This tough, territorial bird often runs other species out of the neighborhood. It's also aggressive toward predators; mockingbirds have been known to dive-bomb cats and snakes. A peculiar feature of mockingbird nests is trash. The birds will build with plastic wrappers, aluminum foil, and even cigarette butts. The female lays two to six eggs per clutch, each about an inch long. They are usually light blue or green with patches of brownish red.

WHERE TO FIND Mockingbirds can be found in wooded areas across the US, in southeastern Canada, and well into northern Mexico. They prefer open woodland areas.

Northern Cardinal (*Cardinalis cardinalis*)

DOMAIN: EUKARYOTA
KINGDOM: ANIMALIA
PHYLUM: CHORDATA
CLASS: AVES
ORDER: PASSERIFORMES
FAMILY: CARDINALIDAE
GENUS: *Cardinalis*
SPECIES: *C. cardinalis*

Northern cardinals have pointed crests atop their heads. The female is brown with red highlights, but it's the male most people enjoy looking at. He's bright red. Even his beak is red. Cardinals are highly territorial, so they fight other cardinals that invade their nesting areas. They even fight their own reflections in windows. They don't seem to learn from that mistake, either. A cardinal sometimes attacks the same window daily for weeks or even months on end. The female lays two to five eggs, each about an inch long. These are usually off-white or light green and speckled with gray or brown.

WHERE TO FIND Cardinals are found across eastern and central US, southeastern Canada, and down into Mexico. They are typically found along woodland edges, gardens, parks, and rural neighborhoods.

HOW TO CANDLE A BIRD'S EGG

The eggs people eat typically don't have chicks developing inside them. Eggs will only contain embryos (developing babies) if the female bird has mated with a male and her eggs have been kept warm (usually with her own body heat; this is called incubation).

How can you tell whether an egg has an embryo inside? The simplest method is called candling. To candle an egg, you'll need a dark room, a bright flashlight, and a friend. Frame the egg with your hands so that no light comes in from the front and back side. Have your friend shine the flashlight through the egg at you. If there's no embryo, you won't see much—just light coming through the egg. (A white chicken egg will produce an orange light.)

If there's an embryo, you may see any of the following:
- Squiggly veins
- A dark mass blocking the light
- An air pocket at one end where the light comes through clearly

An egg with an embryo doesn't preserve well in a cabinet. It may begin to smell, so if you've found a bird egg that contains an embryo, do not try to preserve it for your collection.

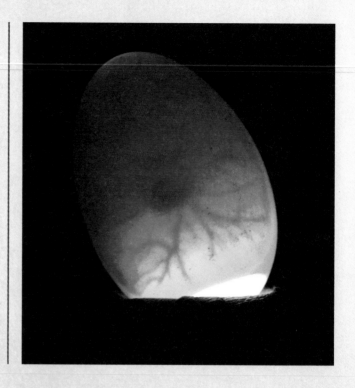

HOW TO PRESERVE A BIRD'S EGG

WHAT YOU NEED:

- A couple of Band-Aids
- A pushpin
- A toothpick
- A skinny straw (The kind used to stir coffee is best.)

1. Put a Band-Aid over each end of the egg. The Band-Aid will help keep it from breaking when you poke holes in it.

2. Use the pin to poke a hole in each end of the egg. Poke right through the Band-Aid and the shell. One hole has to be big enough for a skinny straw to go in. The other has to be big enough to let the goo drip out of the egg.

3. Inside the shell, the gooey parts of the egg are still protected by membranes. Stick a toothpick into the hole and poke around inside. This should break those membranes.

4. Stick a skinny straw in one hole and blow. The goo should blast out the other end of the egg. Keep trying until you can't get any more goo to come out.

5. Hold the egg under a faucet and let water run through it. This will help clean out the rest of the goo. Now, blow through the egg with your straw again to get rid of the leftover water.

6. Find a place for your egg to sit and drain. An empty jar or bottle will work. Just balance the egg on the mouth of the jar or bottle. Make sure one of the holes points straight down so the remaining water can drip out. Leave it there for a couple of days so it dries well.

7. Then, put the egg in a microwave oven for a few seconds. If your shell is the size of a chicken egg, give it about 30 seconds. If it's a swallow's egg, which is smaller than a dime, it only needs about five seconds in the microwave.

CUP NESTS

Birds make different kinds of nests. Some birds, such as wood-peckers, like to carve a hole in a tree and nest inside. Some, like puffins, nest in burrows in cliffs. Some ducks just squat on the ground under a bush and lay eggs. For a collector, the most interesting nests are ones you can actually hold in your hand. These are called cup nests.

Barn Swallow (*Hirundo rustica*)

DOMAIN: EUKARYOTA
KINGDOM: ANIMALIA
PHYLUM: CHORDATA
CLASS: AVES
ORDER: PASSERIFORMES
FAMILY: HIRUNDINIDAE
GENUS: *Hirundo*
SPECIES: *H. rustica*

Barn swallows often make their nests on buildings—not just barns, but any kind of structure that has a place to attach a nest. They lay anywhere from three to seven eggs. Sometimes, if you are careful, you can see the baby birds peeking over the edge of the nest. They open their mouths wide. The inside of a baby swallow's mouth is bright red. The parents know bright red means "feed me."

Usually the mother and father swallows use the nest twice in a year. After the first batch of hatchlings is old enough, the mother lays another batch of eggs. Sometimes the older kids stay around and help feed the new babies. After the second batch the swallows are done with the nest. That means that any nest that has been sitting empty for a year is okay to take. The birds won't want it again. You can collect it without bothering them. It's hard to take the nest, though. Sometimes it is too high to reach safely. Sometimes the nest sticks very tightly to the building. It might even break when you try to take it down. So you should do this carefully with the help of another person.

WHERE TO FIND Barn swallows nest in a variety of habitats, though they prefer being near water and in open country. Since they are often under the eaves of barns and buildings, and beneath bridges and other structures, their nests are generally easy to spot. They can be found across North and South America.

American Goldfinch (*Spinus tristis*)

DOMAIN: EUKARYOTA
KINGDOM: ANIMALIA
PHYLUM: CHORDATA
CLASS: AVES
ORDER: PASSERIFORMES
FAMILY: FRINGILLIDAE
GENUS: *Spinus*
SPECIES: *S. tristis*

The American goldfinch makes its nest with vines, tree bark, weeds, grass, the fluffy parts of cattails and milkweeds, silk from moth cocoons, and spiderweb. Spiderweb is a great building material for birds. It is strong and flexible. It doesn't always seem strong because we usually find it in thin strands. But if you had strands of steel the same thickness as the spiderweb, the spiderweb would be stronger. Sometimes the web is sticky, so it helps hold the nest together.

WHERE TO FIND The American goldfinch can be found from the eastern to western US, and in parts of southern Canada, but it will migrate south in the winter. Its nests can be found in open meadows, weedy fields, floodplains, and orchards, as well as residential areas. It's not uncommon to find a goldfinch nesting in your backyard! They enjoy bird feeders—especially in the wintertime.

TALONS

The claws of birds take different forms depending on the bird's lifestyle. Perching birds use their claws to cling to branches. Gulls use them to hang on to fish. Birds of prey such as eagles, buzzards, owls, and hawks have large, sharp claws called talons for seizing and killing prey.

Common Raven *(Corvus corax)*

DOMAIN: EUKARYOTA
KINGDOM: ANIMALIA
PHYLUM: CHORDATA
CLASS: AVES
ORDER: PASSERIFORMES
FAMILY: CORVIDAE
GENUS: *Corvus*
SPECIES: *C. corax*

Common ravens are big, black birds. They're easily mistaken for crows, but the raven is bigger and has shaggy feathers on its neck and throat. The raven eats an amazing array of food, from human garbage to wolf feces to live lambs. Sometimes the sound of a gun brings ravens out to investigate. They've learned that gunshots sometimes result in dead animals they can eat. Edgar Allan Poe's famous poem "The Raven" has some truth in it: The bird really can be taught to say a few words. The feet and claws of ravens are black, like the rest of its body.

WHERE TO FIND There are many species of raven, which can be found throughout the world. The common raven is found all around the Northern Hemisphere. They prefer wooded areas and coastal regions, often building their nests in sea cliffs.

Bald Eagle *(Haliaeetus leucocephalus)*

DOMAIN: EUKARYOTA
KINGDOM: ANIMALIA
PHYLUM: CHORDATA
CLASS: AVES
ORDER: ACCIPITRIFORMES
FAMILY: ACCIPITRIDAE
GENUS: *Haliaeetus*
SPECIES: *H. leucocephalus*

The bald eagle can dive off a cliff to snatch a fish from the water and come flying out. It prefers easier methods, though. It will harass smaller birds into dropping their prey, then snatch the prey for itself. It will even snatch a live fish from a fisherman's line. In the past, the species was endangered because humans hunted and poisoned it. Under government protection, its numbers rebounded to healthy levels in most of the US. The bald eagle has brown feathers on its body and white ones on its head. Its hooked beak and powerful feet are yellow.

WHERE TO FIND The bald eagle can be found throughout North America, including most of Canada and northern Mexico. It typically lives near large bodies of water, so they can be spotted along seacoasts, large lakes, and wide rivers.

THE BALD EAGLE IS THE NATIONAL SYMBOL OF THE UNITED STATES OF AMERICA.

BEAKS

The beak, or bill, is the tough, specialized mouth gear of a bird. Inside the beak are the jawbones. The jawbones are covered with skin. The top layer of skin is what makes the beak different from the jaws of most vertebrates. That layer is strengthened with keratin, the same protein found in nails and claws. Beaks come in a huge variety of shapes, depending on how different birds have evolved to use them. For example, many songbirds have small beaks with serrated edges for gripping and cracking seeds. Ducks, on the other hand, have fairly wide beaks because they use them to probe mud for food. Ducks even have a special nail on the beak to help them pry mollusks off rocks.

Macaw (family Psittacidae)

DOMAIN: EUKARYOTA
KINGDOM: ANIMALIA
PHYLUM: CHORDATA
CLASS: AVES
ORDER: PSITTACIFORMES
FAMILY: PSITTACIDAE

Six genera of parrots are known as macaws. What sets them apart from other parrots is a long tail, a pattern of light patches on the face, and a big beak. The macaw uses that powerful beak to crack the nuts and seeds it eats. It also eats the flowers, fruit, leaves, and stems of various plants. Some of those items are poisonous to other animals, but the macaw is immune. In some places, macaws also eat clay from riverbanks, probably to get nutrients they can't get from the plants they eat.

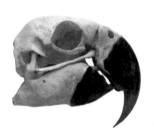

WHERE TO FIND There are seventeen species of macaws, all of which live in Central and South America.

Cuckoo (family Cuculidae)

DOMAIN: EUKARYOTA
KINGDOM: ANIMALIA
PHYLUM: CHORDATA
CLASS: AVES
ORDER: CUCULIFORMES
FAMILY: CUCULIDAE

A common cuckoo hen doesn't make a nest for her eggs. Instead, she visits some other bird's nest while it's not home. She shoves one of its eggs out of the nest and lays one of her own to replace it. If the other bird doesn't notice the switch, it will incubate the imposter egg and then feed the cuckoo that hatches out of it. The young cuckoo gets more food for itself by shoving the other eggs and hatchlings out of the nest if it can. This imposter-egg strategy is called brood parasitism. When they're not busy fooling other birds, cuckoos eat insects. They specialize in poisonous caterpillars that other birds won't eat. To avoid the poison, the cuckoo slices the caterpillar open and shakes the poison out. Its straight, sharp beak is ideal for this work.

WHERE TO FIND Cuckoos can be found all over the world, although they prefer a mild climate.

OWL PELLETS

A bird pellet looks something like a pill or a ball measuring up to two inches. It is usually brown or gray. If you break it open, you'll find a mess inside. There might be broken seed coverings, bark, fur, insect parts, or even tiny bones.

Where does this little parcel of parts come from?

A bird regurgitated it. In other words, the bird puked it up.

When a person throws up, it means he or she is sick. But for many species of birds, it's normal. They regurgitate as a way of getting rid of things they can't digest. For example, a bird might eat a seed with a tough covering. The inside of the seed is nutritious food. The tough covering isn't, so the bird just spits it up. Along with the indigestible food, the bird is also spitting out harmful germs that may have formed inside its digestive system.

Scientists like to study pellets. By breaking them apart, the scientists can tell what the bird has been eating. Sometimes they find surprising things, like the talons of a smaller bird.

Pellets are fun to collect. It's especially cool if you can recognize bones or fur in them. The most popular pellets to collect are owl pellets. Owls (order Strigiformes) eat other animals. Sometimes you can find the bones of mice or rats in their pellets. Sometimes you will see fur. Usually, you can't tell what mammal the fur came from. It could be from a rabbit, a squirrel, a bat, or a weasel. It could even be from a skunk. Owls are the only birds that prey on skunks. One scientist saw an owl kill

OWLS CAN VARY GREATLY IN SIZE. ONE OF THE LARGEST, THE EURASIAN EAGLE-OWL, CAN GROW TO 30 INCHES. THE SMALLEST OWL, THE ELF OWL, IS ONLY ABOUT 5 INCHES LONG.

a skunk by squeezing its head until its skull broke. Another scientist found parts of fifty-seven skunks in one owl's nest.

You might also find feathers. Big owls eat many kinds of birds, from crows to woodpeckers to ducks. Sometimes they even eat other predators, like the red-tailed hawk. When an owl eats another bird, it tears off the wings and most of the feathers and throws them away. But sometimes it accidentally swallows a few feathers. That's why they end up in the pellet.

You might think pellets sound disgusting. They usually aren't too gross, though. Often, they dry out, so they are not slimy. They can smell bad, but not as bad as human vomit. The only thing to be careful about is germs. Some of the animals a bird might eat carry diseases that can affect people. For example, mice can spread a virus that causes a form of meningitis. To kill such germs, you should cook the pellet in a microwave oven. (Just check with the rest of your household first.) It needs to be cooked for twenty seconds on the "high" setting. This goes for any bird pellets you find in the wild. If you buy owl pellets, the store will usually have cooked them already.

After you are through looking at the pellet, you can put it all in a small jar or vial that will fit in your cabinet. Or, you can simply use a see-through plastic bag. You can also put in a slip of paper that tells what you found. For example, you might write "Pellet from an Unknown Bird. Contains grasshopper parts." That way, other people can tell what it is.

WHERE TO FIND Owls can be found in every corner of the earth, with the exception of Antarctica. Hence, owl pellets can be found everywhere, too. It's best to look for them near locations where owls perch.

HOW TO DISSECT AN OWL PELLET

To see what's inside an owl pellet, you can break it apart with tweezers and a fork. You might also like to buy a dissecting kit. This is a little plastic box that holds tools useful for cutting up animals and plants. A typical kit holds tweezers, scissors, long metal pins, a scalpel, and a ruler. It also has some handy tools called dissecting probes. These are simply sticks with sharp metal pokers on the end. You can use them to carefully tear open cocoons and dead bugs as well as pellets.

REPTILIA
(REPTILES)

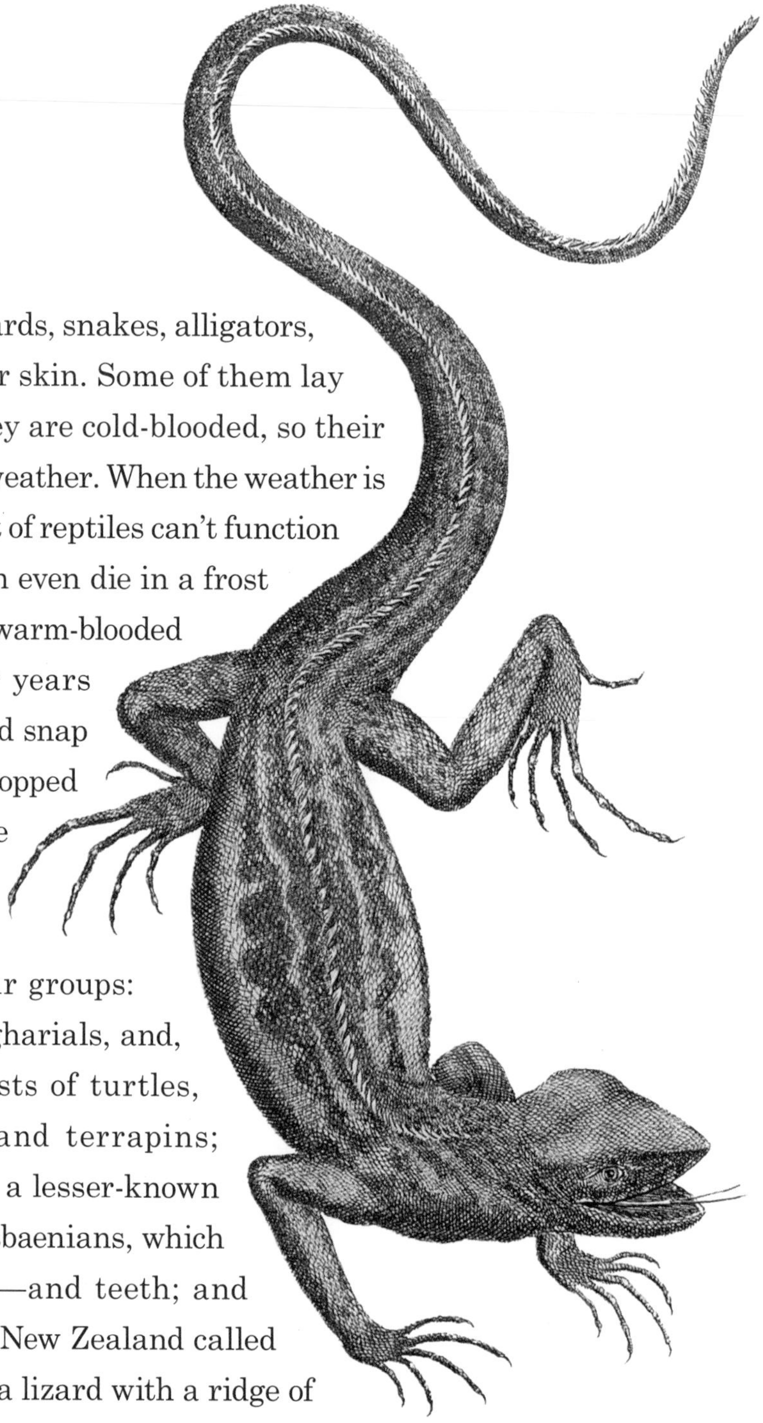

Reptiles—animals such as turtles, lizards, snakes, alligators, and crocodiles—have scales on their skin. Some of them lay eggs; others give birth to live young. They are cold-blooded, so their bodies get warm or cold depending on the weather. When the weather is hot, they move around with ease. But a lot of reptiles can't function in the cold. They become sluggish and can even die in a frost that wouldn't cause many problems for a warm-blooded mammal or bird. That happened a few years ago in Florida, when an unseasonable cold snap killed hundreds of wild iguanas. They dropped from the trees like ripe apples. To cope with the cold, some reptiles sleep, or hibernate, through the winter.

Modern reptiles are divided into four groups: Crocodilia includes alligators, caimans, gharials, and, of course, crocodiles; Testudines consists of turtles, including those known as tortoises and terrapins; Squamata includes lizards, snakes, and a lesser-known group of burrowing reptiles called amphisbaenians, which look like worms with loose, scaly skin—and teeth; and Sphenodontia includes only reptiles from New Zealand called tuatara. At a glance, a tuatara looks like a lizard with a ridge of spines running down its back. A closer examination shows some differences from lizards. It has two rows of teeth on top and one on the bottom. It also has a noticeable third eye in the middle of its head. Some lizards (as well as frogs) also have third eyes, but they're so small that people rarely notice them.

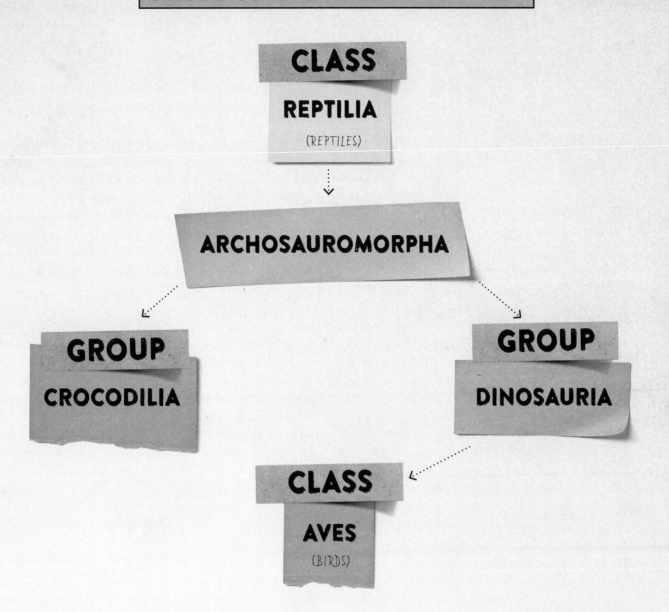

CLASS

REPTILIA

(REPTILES)

ARCHOSAUROMORPHA

GROUP

CROCODILIA

GROUP

DINOSAURIA

CLASS

AVES

(BIRDS)

Scientists first split reptiles into a separate group almost two hundred years ago. Then, as they studied the forms of the animals, they divided all living reptiles into the groups described on the previous page. They established other groups, too, to include extinct reptiles such as dinosaurs. As it turns out, the whole class was a huge mistake.

Scientists are always working to improve taxonomy, and as a result, they've changed many groupings over the years. For example, we now know that cheetahs and cougars are closely related; they belong to the same lineage within the larger cat family. That's an important change for biologists who specialize in cats, but it's no big deal for the rest of us. The key to this particular change, and many others that have happened in just the last couple of decades, is genetic evidence. By comparing DNA, scientists have been able to figure out evolutionary relationships with far greater precision than ever before.

Something similar happened with Reptilia, thanks to fossil discoveries, as well as genetic evidence. In this case, though, the new information forces scientists and everybody else into a new understanding of a whole class of animals. It's a confusing situation, but it also makes this an exciting time to study animals.

Scientists now arrange our four groups of living reptiles, along with dinosaurs and birds, inside three broader clades:

Testudines: The turtles. So far, no problem; this is exactly the same as a group we already used under the old system. Plus, anybody can tell at a glance that all the shelled reptiles are related.

Lepidosauromorpha: The squamates (lizards, snakes, and amphisbaenians); the sphenodonts (tuatara); and various extinct reptiles. Still no problem; this is simply a big group that puts together smaller groups we already knew about.

Archosauromorpha: The crocodilians, the dinosaurs and certain other extinct reptiles, and the birds. Here's the problem: Common sense and centuries of habit tell us that birds are quite different from reptiles. But they're actually not; they evolved from a certain group of dinosaurs. Some of those dinosaurs even had feathers. So the birds are a subset of dinosaurs, which are themselves a subset of reptiles.

TURTLE SHELLS

A turtle's shell doesn't come off; it's part of the turtle's body. The shell is mostly made of bone. After a turtle dies, its shell can last centuries—or, in the right conditions, millions of years. The shell has two parts. The top part, which covers the turtle's back, is called a carapace. The bottom part, which covers the turtle's chest and belly, is called a plastron. What sets the turtles apart from all other reptiles is the shell. Those durable shells have been discovered in fossils that are more than 200 million years old. They preserve so well that they are sometimes found by the thousands in "turtle graveyards." These are ancient ponds or lakes that dried up and left many turtles to die in the same place at about the same time.

You'll hear several different terms used for turtles. In scientific usage, a "tortoise" is a land-living turtle of the family Testudinidae. Tortoises have tall, domed shells and thick legs made for walking on land. "Terrapin" is used for several edible species of freshwater turtles, some of which are not closely related to each other. All tortoises and terrapins belong to the larger group Testudines, so it's always scientifically accurate to call them turtles.

HOW TO PRESERVE A TORTOISE OR TURTLE SHELL

It's possible to find a plastron or a carapace separately. Or, you might find a whole shell.

METHOD 1

If you find a shell in the wild, you should leave it outside until insects and germs eat away all the flesh. You'll know it's ready to collect when it no longer smells. This can take months.

METHOD 2

If you don't have a place outdoors to let the flesh decompose naturally, you can speed things up by cooking the meat off the turtle on your stove. Be warned: This method stinks—literally. I don't recommend it for a large turtle.

1. Loosen the meat by boiling, then leave simmering for a few hours. Let cool.

2. With an old toothbrush, scrub away the rest of the meat.

3. Boil again. Allow to cool.

4. Fill the shell with borax (use caution) or salt and let it sit on a plate for a couple of hours.

5. Empty the shell and scrub it again.

6. Once the shell is dry, use ordinary school glue to re-attach any scales that have fallen off.

7. (Optional) Paint the shell with clear polyurethane to preserve it and give it a bright finish.

African Spurred Tortoise
(*Centrochelys sulcata*)

DOMAIN: EUKARYOTA
KINGDOM: ANIMALIA
PHYLUM: CHORDATA
CLASS: REPTILIA
ORDER: TESTUDINES
FAMILY: TESTUDINIDAE
GENUS: *Centrochelys*
SPECIES: *C. sulcata*

This grass-eating species can grow to an impressive size—up to 3 feet long and 200 pounds. That makes it the third-largest kind of tortoise. It is often kept as a pet because of its beautiful shell, which has lighter-colored pyramids jutting out from the main body of the carapace like hills from a landscape.

WHERE TO FIND Native to the Sahara Desert and the semiarid grasslands of Sahel, the African spurred tortoise can be found in various arid regions throughout Africa.

Red-Footed Tortoise
(*Chelonoidis carbonaria*)

DOMAIN: EUKARYOTA
KINGDOM: ANIMALIA
PHYLUM: CHORDATA
CLASS: REPTILIA
ORDER: TESTUDINES
FAMILY: TESTUDINIDAE
GENUS: *Chelonoidis*
SPECIES: *C. carbonaria*

This South American species is an omnivore—it likes fruit, mushrooms, worms, insects, and even carrion, or dead animals. The dark skin of its head and legs is speckled with a brighter color—yellow, orange, or the glowing-coal red that gives the species its common name. The adults average about 12 to 14 inches in length, so the shell is large. Its colors vary quite a bit. Generally, the shell is dark, with a lighter patch in the middle of each big scute, or scale. The lighter patch may match the speckles on the tortoise's legs—the ones with red patches are especially attractive.

WHERE TO FIND While the red-footed tortoise is native to northern South America and several islands in the Caribbean, it is found fairly easily in the US, where it is a common pet.

Asian Leaf Turtle
(*Cyclemys dentata* and its close relatives)

DOMAIN: EUKARYOTA
KINGDOM: ANIMALIA
PHYLUM: CHORDATA
CLASS: REPTILIA
ORDER: TESTUDINES
FAMILY: GEOEMYDIDAE
GENUS: *Cyclemys*
SPECIES: *C. dentata*

These omnivorous turtles live near slow forest streams and ponds. Their meat makes for good eating, and fishermen often catch them for that purpose. The fishermen have to be careful, though, because a leaf turtle defends itself by vomiting on an attacker. It grows to around 10 inches. Its shell is a richly textured brown or green. It's called a "leaf" turtle because some people think its shell looks like a round leaf.

WHERE TO FIND The Asian leaf turtle is native to Southeast Asia.

CROCODILE SKULLS

Crocodilians form an order (Crocodilia) of large swimming predators. Because they often ambush their prey from the water, their eyes, nostrils, and ears are on top of their heads. This allows them to float unseen while watching, smelling, and listening for prey. Their sense of touch also helps them hunt: The nerves in their faces are incredibly sensitive to vibration and can detect the motions of other animals in the water. The flat, heavily muscled skull of a crocodilian can bite with more force than almost any other animal. The biggest crocodiles can even bite and drag down powerful prey like horses and rhinoceroses—and not-so-powerful prey like humans.

The twenty-four species of crocodilians fall into three families:

Gavialidae: The gharials
Alligatoridae: The alligators and caimans
Crocodylidae: The crocodiles

How do you tell them apart? With the gharials, it's easy. They specialize in fish, so they have long, slender snouts shaped like the handles of pans that allow them to snap rapidly in water. With the rest, it's more difficult because there are so many species, each with its own size, shape, color pattern, and other traits. Also, individual animals vary in appearance. (People often get to know the local crocodilians and even name them.)

In general, alligators and caimans have broad, rounded snouts. When their mouths are closed, their teeth don't show that much.

Crocodiles typically have narrower, pointy snouts. With its mouth closed, the fourth tooth on both sides of a croc's lower jaw shows.

HOW AN ALLIGATOR EATS

How does an alligator catch and eat its prey? First of all, it uses its strong jaws to clamp on to its prey. Its teeth don't have to be very sharp. The jaws are strong enough to drive even blunt teeth through flesh. They can break through turtle shells or mammal bones. The alligator may then swallow its prey whole.

If it's too big to swallow whole, the alligator may use a tactic called the death roll. In a death roll, the alligator holds on to the prey and spins its own body. It flops from its belly to its back and then to its belly again. All the time, it holds on to the prey. The motion tears off a piece of the prey—say, its leg. The alligator swallows the pieces.

Another trick for breaking the prey into pieces is to drag it underwater and leave it there. The alligator crams the dead animal into a crag among rocks or under floating logs. After a few days, the prey decays enough to soften. Then the alligator can tear it apart easily.

Inside the alligator's stomach, more interesting things happen. The alligator swallows a few small rocks. Once inside, the rocks bump against the prey over and over, grinding it up. It's like having teeth inside the gut.

Most animals' stomachs make acid that helps digest their food. The strongest of all stomach acids is found in alligators and their relatives. That's why they can eat big chunks of meat without needing to chew them.

American Alligator (Alligator mississippiensis)

DOMAIN: EUKARYOTA
KINGDOM: ANIMALIA
PHYLUM: CHORDATA
CLASS: REPTILIA
ORDER: CROCODILIA
FAMILY: ALLIGATORIDAE
GENUS: Alligator
SPECIES: A. mississippiensis

An alligator's skull has one simple kind of teeth. These teeth can't do any of the special jobs mammal teeth can. They can't take a bite out of an apple, like a person can. They can't shear off a big chunk of flesh, like a carnivoran can. They can't grind down plants, like a cow does. You might expect an alligator to have sharp teeth, but it doesn't. Its teeth are sharp enough to hold on to prey, but not nearly as sharp as a fox's or a skunk's. They're more like blunt cones.

WHERE TO FIND American alligators can be found in swamps, lakes, and rivers all along the southeastern US, and west to the southern tip of Texas.

Saltwater Crocodile (Crocodylus porosus)

DOMAIN: EUKARYOTA
KINGDOM: ANIMALIA
PHYLUM: CHORDATA
SUBPHYLUM: VERTEBRATA
CLASS: REPTILIA
ORDER: CROCODILIA
FAMILY: CROCODYLIDAE
GENUS: Crocodylus
SPECIES: C. porosus

The saltwater crocodile is the largest reptile in the world. It can grow to 22 feet and weigh more than two tons. It's also the most dangerous, rivaled only by the Nile crocodile. Partly that's because of its size, but it's also more aggressive than most other crocodilians. It has been known to attack people who are wading, swimming, or snorkeling. On a couple of occasions, a "saltie" has even come into a person's tent. Its skull can be huge—sometimes more than 30 inches long.

WHERE TO FIND Although saltwater crocodiles can live in salt water, they are more typically found in swamps, lagoons, and rivers in India, Southeast Asia, and Australia.

SNAKE SKIN, BONES, and TAILS

The skin of a snake is covered with thousands of small, hard plates called scales. The scales overlap to protect the tender skin beneath. The shape of the scales varies with the type of snake, and each snake has different kinds of scales on different parts of its body. In rattlesnakes, for example, the scales on the back are shaped like flattened sunflower seeds. Underneath, however, each scale goes all the way across the belly, like a set of pale stripes. Unless the snake has recently been in the water or molted, its skin is dry, not slimy as some people think.

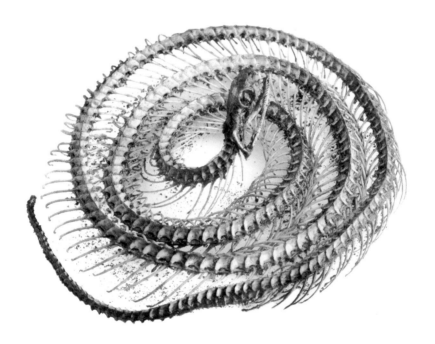

Snake SKELETON (suborder Serpentes)

DOMAIN: EUKARYOTA
KINGDOM: ANIMALIA
PHYLUM: CHORDATA
CLASS: REPTILIA
ORDER: SQUAMATA
SUBORDER: SERPENTES

A snake's skeleton is made up of a skull and jawbones, a small throat-bone called the hyoid, a spine, and ribs. The spine is a string of small bones called vertebrae (that's the plural form; an individual piece is called a vertebra). Each vertebra in a snake's back has two ribs attached to it, one sticking out on each side. The back merges smoothly into the tail, but the vertebrae in the tail have no ribs. The ribs of most snakes are tiny, thinner than needles. Snakes evolved from lizards, and this fact is still visible in the skeletons of a few snakes, such as some pythons. The pythons have spurs near their back ends. These spurs are the vestiges of hind legs.

WHERE TO FIND Snakes can be found nearly everywhere on earth except Antarctica, Ireland, or Iceland. You can find snake skeletons wherever there are living snakes: grasslands, wetlands, caves, deserts, rivers, mountains, forests, and savannas.

Snake SKIN (suborder Serpentes)

DOMAIN: EUKARYOTA
KINGDOM: ANIMALIA
PHYLUM: CHORDATA
CLASS: REPTILIA
ORDER: SQUAMATA
SUBORDER: SERPENTES

Snakes molt, or shed their skin. They molt so that they can grow bigger. The more a snake eats, the more often it needs to molt. When a snake is ready to molt, its skin becomes milky white and its eyes turn a milky blue. The snake can't move very easily when it is molting, so it may hide. The snake gets the old skin to come off by rubbing against plants, rocks, or whatever it can find. The new skin, which has already formed underneath the old one, emerges sleek and moist. In comparison, the old one looks as faded as a scuffed shoe.

The shed skin of a snake feels soft and slightly crisp, like a cheese puff. It will break if you handle it roughly. Sometimes the old skin breaks into many pieces when it comes off. A whole shed is a more desirable find. It allows you to see the shape of the snake.

WHERE TO FIND Snake skins are found anywhere snakes live, but can be fragile, so take care.

Rattlesnake TAIL (genus *Sistrurus*)

DOMAIN: EUKARYOTA
KINGDOM: ANIMALIA
PHYLUM: CHORDATA
CLASS: REPTILIA
ORDER: SQUAMATA
SUBORDER: SERPENTES
FAMILY: VIPERIDAE
GENUS: *Sistrurus*

Many snakes warn away predators by shaking their tails against leaves to make a noise, but rattlesnakes are the only ones that have special equipment for making this racket. If a predator, or any animal that happens to get too close, doesn't back off when the snake rattles, it may bite with its two hollow fangs, which can inject a dangerous venom. The venom can be fatal to humans. The rattle grows with each molt. It's made of keratin and feels like human fingernails.

WHERE TO FIND Rattlesnakes are only found in North and South America, from southern Canada to Argentina.

OSTEICHTHYES (BONY FISH) AND CHONDRICHTHYES (CARTILAGINOUS FISH)

Fish are ancient creatures: Fossil evidence suggests both major groups existed more than 400 million years ago. By comparison, reptiles appeared less than 320 million years ago. Dinosaurs appeared only 231 million years ago, and mammals less than 200 million years ago. With over 28,000 living species, bony fish form the largest class of vertebrates.

BONY and CARTILAGINOUS FISH

There are two main kinds of fish: cartilaginous and bony. In taxonomic ranking, this differentiation comes between phylum and class and is called a superclass. Cartilaginous fish do not have bones except in their jaws. Their skeletons are made of cartilage, which is a tough, flexible kind of tissue. (Your ear is mostly made of cartilage.) The cartilaginous fish include sharks, stingrays, and manta rays, among others.

Bony fish have skeletons made of bone as well as cartilage, just like mammals and birds and reptiles do. Most kinds of fish you hear about are bony fish—tuna, trout, goldfish, bettas, cod, herring, gar, pike, swordfish, and approximately 28,000 more.

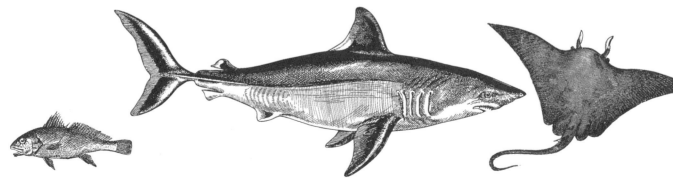

Osteichthyes are fish that have skeletons made of bones, which includes tens of thousands of species.

Chondrichthyes are fish that have skeletons made of cartilage, which includes all sharks and rays.

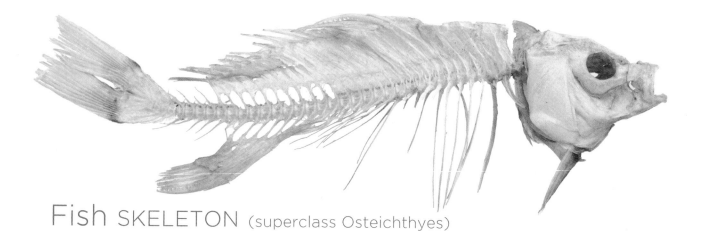

Fish SKELETON (superclass Osteichthyes)

DOMAIN: EUKARYOTA
KINGDOM: ANIMALIA
PHYLUM: CHORDATA
SUPERCLASS: OSTEICHTHYES

The bones of fish can be hard to preserve, but they're actually pretty easy to find. Just open a can of salmon and you'll find ribs and pieces of backbone. But the bones can be so small that people and animals simply eat them with the meat.

With most fish, the skull, jaw, and vertebrae last after the rest of the body has dried out. There may also be the bones of the fins and tail. It's not unusual to find some scaly skin attached to the bones. Unless it is completely dry, it's best to scrape off any skin to avoid rot.

WHERE TO FIND Fish are found everywhere in the world: in oceans, rivers, streams, and lakes.

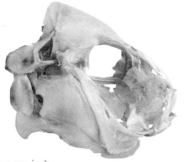

Carp SKULL (*Cyprinus carpio*)

DOMAIN: EUKARYOTA
KINGDOM: ANIMALIA
PHYLUM: CHORDATA
SUPERCLASS: OSTEICHTHYES
CLASS: ACTINOPTERYGII
ORDER: CYPRINIFORMES
FAMILY: CYPRINIDAE
GENUS: *Cyprinus*
SPECIES: *C. carpio*

Most people don't eat the heads of fish, so they often get tossed aside. It's easy to find them wherever a lot of people go fishing. You can look around such places and pick up the heads that have dried out. Microwave them for a minute when you get home, to make sure you've killed all the germs.

Fish heads of most species make interesting specimens. Let's consider the head of a common carp (*Cyprinus carpio*), for example. A good-size specimen will be broader and longer than your hand. You will also see the gills.

Gills are what fish use to breathe. Most fish don't have lungs like ours. They breathe through complicated filters on the sides of their heads. These filters—the gills—take oxygen from the water. In a live fish, the gills look like a set of venetian blinds. They open and close as the fish breathes. Inside the living fish, the gills are made of comblike bones covered with red flesh. In a dried carp head, nothing is left but a flat piece of bone that looks like an open fan.

Depending on how far back the head was chopped, you may also be able to see some of the scales and spine. The scales of the carp cover most of its body behind the head. The scales feel like dead leaves. They break easily.

WHERE TO FIND Although originally from Asia, the common carp's hardiness and ability to adapt to different environments have helped it spread across the globe. Carp can now be found everywhere in the world.

Sea Horse (genus *Hippocampus*)

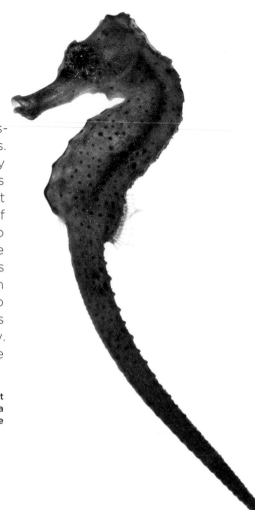

DOMAIN: EUKARYOTA
KINGDOM: ANIMALIA
PHYLUM: CHORDATA
CLASS: ACTINOPTERYGII
ORDER: GASTEROSTEIFORMES
FAMILY: SYNGNATHIDAE
GENUS: *Hippocampus*

Sea horses are predators that ambush tiny crustaceans and suck them up with their long snouts. They have several features unusual among bony fish: a distinct neck, which is part of what makes them look like horses; a tail that's prehensile—that is, capable of grasping things, such as stalks of plants; and a vertical body (most fish are built to swim horizontally). Another unusual feature is the pouch on the male's belly. The female lays eggs directly into the pouch and the male carries them until the hatchlings are ready to be released into the water. An important feature for collectors is the bony rings that structure the sea horse's body. These rings cause the sea horse to keep its shape even after it dries out.

WHERE TO FIND Sea horses are found in tropical waters throughout the world, preferring coral reefs and sheltered areas. The slender sea horse, pictured here, can be found in the southern US and along the coastal waters of Central America and northern South America.

Alligator Gar Fish SCALES (*Atractosteus spatula*)

DOMAIN: EUKARYOTA
KINGDOM: ANIMALIA
PHYLUM: CHORDATA
CLASS: ACTINOPTERYGII
ORDER: SEMIONOTIFORMES
FAMILY: LEPISOSTEIDAE
GENUS: *Atractosteus*
SPECIES: *A. spatula*

Alligator gar are fish that can grow to be 10 feet long and weigh more than 300 pounds. They are usually the biggest fish found in the rivers and lakes of the US. They look a lot like alligators, with a long, toothy snout and a long body. But instead of legs, they have fins. They eat turtles, small mammals, ducks, and other fish. They are so big that almost nothing preys on them. Their only enemies are actual alligators and humans. People catch them with a net, a rod and reel, or a bow and arrow.

The scales that cover an alligator gar are collectible. Beneath the skin, they're made of a gleaming white material. Each scale is shaped like a diamond, mostly flat but thicker in the middle. That thick middle is as hard and smooth as a tooth. The fluted edges have a little give to them, like stiff plastic. A small scale is about the size of your fingertip; a big one is wider and longer than a playing card.

It's no wonder the scales feel like teeth. They are actually coated with enamel, like the teeth of humans and sharks.

WHERE TO FIND Alligator gars are mostly found in rivers, reservoirs, and lakes of the southern US and sometimes in the Gulf of Mexico. They are most common in Texas, Louisiana, and throughout the lower Mississippi River Valley.

HOW TO PRESERVE The scales have to be scrubbed clean. After that, you don't have to do anything special to preserve them. They will last as long as teeth or bones.

Great White Shark TOOTH (*Carcharodon carcharias*)

DOMAIN: EUKARYOTA
KINGDOM: ANIMALIA
PHYLUM: CHORDATA
CLASS: CHONDRICHTHYES
ORDER: LAMNIFORMES
FAMILY: LAMNIDAE
GENUS: *Carcharodon*
SPECIES: *C. carcharias*

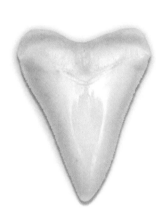

The great white shark has about three thousand teeth to bite with at any time. It also has new rows of teeth growing behind those. That's necessary because it loses a lot of teeth. The great white's teeth are not planted in its jaws, like human teeth are. They grow out of the cartilage in its gums. It doesn't take much to pull them out. Over the course of its life, the great white shark loses tens of thousands of teeth. It never runs out.

The shark's body is covered with scales. Each scale has a fleshy core called the pulp, which contains blood vessels and nerves. Surrounding the pulp is a bony substance called dentine. Surrounding the dentine is a hard coating that protects the scale. These scales are so much like teeth that a shark can often make a prey animal bleed just by bumping it.

The shark's actual teeth have an even stronger protective coating. They are made of smooth enamel just like human teeth. It's the hardest substance in our bodies—harder than bone. It is also the hardest substance in the shark's body.

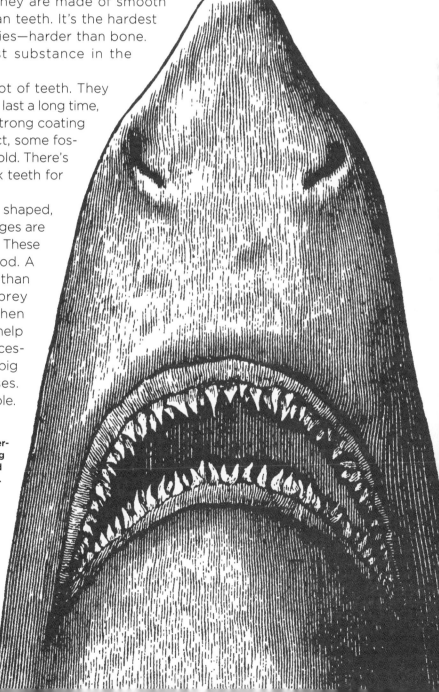

So a shark has a lot of teeth. They fall out easily, and they last a long time, because they have a strong coating to protect them. In fact, some fossilized shark teeth are 450 million years old. There's a good chance you can find some shark teeth for your cabinet.

Great white shark teeth are triangle shaped, and can be up to 5 inches long. Their edges are serrated, with many small, sharp notches. These notches help the shark saw through food. A great white's lower teeth are narrower than its top ones. They mostly hold their prey while the top teeth saw through it. When it attacks, the shark shakes its head to help with the sawing. All of this sawing is necessary because great whites prey on some big animals, like elephant seals and walruses. Those animals are too big to swallow whole. They have to be eaten in chunks.

WHERE TO FIND Great white sharks live in water temperatures between 54°F and 75°F, and can be found along the Atlantic northeast and Pacific coasts of the US, and in Hawaii, Japan, Oceania, Chile, and the Mediterranean. They are also found in abundance along the coast of South Africa and Australia.

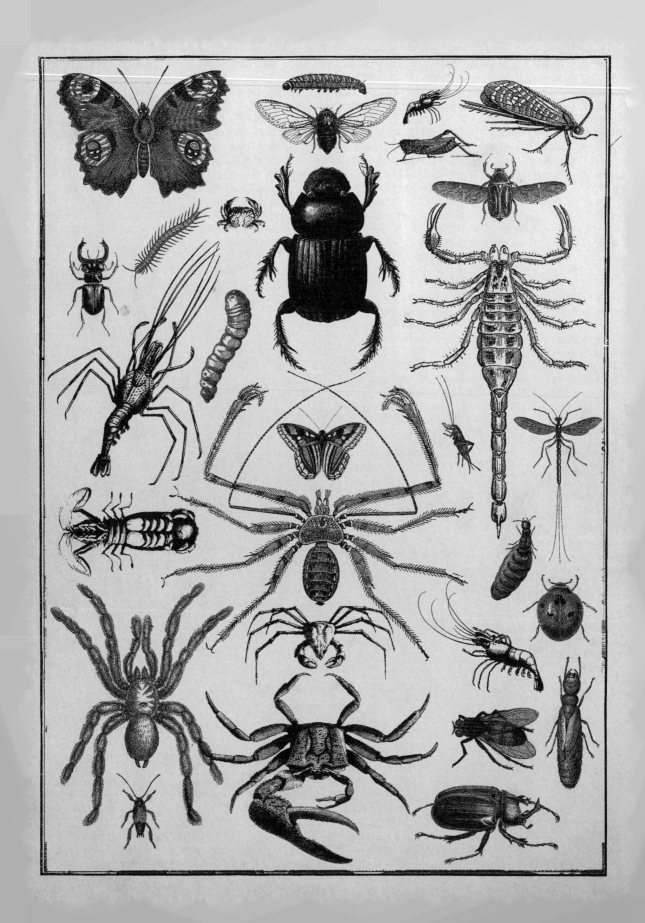

CHAPTER THREE

PHYLUM
ARTHROPODA

Arthropods are invertebrates, which means they don't have backbones. Their bodies have exoskeletons—an external, shell-like coating instead of bones—and are segmented into different parts. They also have limbs with joints.

The main arthropod groups are these: arachnids (spiders, scorpions, mites, ticks, and their relatives); crustaceans (crabs, lobsters, shrimp, and many other kinds of mostly aquatic animals); myriapods (arthropods with long, wormlike bodies and dozens of legs, including centipedes, millipedes, and others); and insects (six-legged arthropods whose life cycle includes a metamorphosis, such as butterflies, beetles, grasshoppers, flies, and many more).

Scientists have cataloged more than one million species of arthropods. There are probably a great many more yet to be discovered. In most places on earth, the arthropods far outnumber all other animals.

CLASS

INSECTA
(INSECTS)

What's the difference between insects and other arthropods? First of all, an insect has six legs. Spiders (arachnids) have eight legs. Centipedes (chilopods) have dozens (the exact number varies). When you are counting the legs of an insect, be sure not to count the antennae. Antennae are feelers attached to the insect's head.

Second, an insect has three main body sections: the head, the thorax, and the abdomen. On the head are the insect's mouth and any eyes it has, plus the antennae. The thorax is the middle part of the body. Besides the legs, it is also where any wings are attached. The abdomen is the back part of the body. It holds many of the important organs, like the lungs and the heart.

Like all arthropods, an insect has an exoskeleton. When an insect grows bigger, it develops a new, larger exoskeleton under its old one. Then the old one splits open and the insect takes it off, like a person taking off his or her clothes.

All insects change their shape as they grow up. This change is called metamorphosis. Some insects have a complete metamorphosis. That means they go through four different stages as they grow up: egg, larva, pupa, and imago. The house fly is a good example. First, it is an egg. When it hatches out of its egg, it is a wormlike larva. (A fly larva is called a maggot.) Later, it turns into a smooth, oval pupa. A pupa mostly stays still as its body changes shape. Finally, it sheds its pupa exoskeleton and comes out as an adult fly. An adult insect is called an imago.

Other insects have an incomplete metamorphosis. That means they only go through three stages as they grow up: egg, nymph, and imago. A grasshopper is a good example. As soon as it comes out of its egg, it is a nymph. The nymph looks pretty much like a grown-up grasshopper, but smaller. The main difference you can see between a grasshopper nymph and the imago is that the imago has wings.

There are millions of kinds of insects. Some scientists think there are more insects than any other kind of living thing. You can collect insects for years and still find new ones.

BUTTERFLIES and MOTHS

Butterflies and moths have a complete metamorphosis—they go from egg to larva to pupa to imago. In their case, the larva is called a caterpillar. When the caterpillar of a moth is ready to become a pupa, it spins a cocoon—a soft bag made of silk. The moth pulls the liquid silk out of its body. The strands quickly solidify in the air. The moth changes into a pupa inside its cocoon. Instead of a cocoon, a butterfly caterpillar simply develops a hard, shell-like exoskeleton when it is ready to pupate. A butterfly pupa in its hard exoskeleton is called a chrysalis.

When a pupa turns into an imago, it comes out of its cocoon or its chrysalis shell. After resting for a while and unfolding its wings, it flies away.

Even in their imago stage, you can usually tell the difference between butterflies and moths. Here are some clues to look for:

• Each of a butterfly's antennae looks like a string with a ball at the end. They are said to be "clubbed."

• Moth antennae can come in many shapes, from stringy to comblike, as with the emperor moth shown here, but they are almost never clubbed.

• A butterfly's body tends to be slender and smooth.

• A moth's body is thick and furry.

• A butterfly flies around in the day.

• A moth flies around in the night.

Eastern Tiger Swallowtail Butterfly

(Papilio glaucus)

DOMAIN: EUKARYOTA
KINGDOM: ANIMALIA
PHYLUM: ARTHROPODA
CLASS: INSECTA
ORDER: LEPIDOPTERA
FAMILY: PAPILIONIDAE
GENUS: *Papilio*
SPECIES: *P. glaucus*

Why are they called swallowtails? Because they have a sort of tail on each wing that pokes out behind as they fly, much like the birds called swallows.

Male tiger swallowtails look very different from females. The female has black front wings with white dots along the edges. Her back wings are a shiny blue, with more white dots on the edges. The male has bright yellow wings with black stripes. He's colored a little bit like a tiger—that's where that part of the name comes from. Most people wouldn't guess that these two butterflies are the same species. If you've already read the birds section of this book, you may remember a term for that: sexual dimorphism. (Another example of sexual dimorphism is the lion. A male lion usually has a mane of hair on his head and neck. Female lions don't.)

WHERE TO FIND Eastern tiger swallowtail butterflies can be found in fields, gardens, parks, and forests throughout the eastern US, from southern Vermont to northern Florida, and as far west as Texas and the Great Plains.

Monarch Butterfly

(Danaus plexippus)

DOMAIN: EUKARYOTA
KINGDOM: ANIMALIA
PHYLUM: ARTHROPODA
CLASS: INSECTA
ORDER: LEPIDOPTERA
FAMILY: NYMPHALIDAE
GENUS: *Danaus*
SPECIES: *D. plexippus*

Monarch butterflies have bright orange wings veined and framed with black. This scheme of black with orange (or red) warns birds and other predators that the butterfly tastes bad. Similar colors occur in many unrelated animals that are toxic, including spiders and even birds. They also occur in a few harmless species, such as other butterflies that benefit from their resemblance to the distasteful monarch. The monarch acquires that nasty taste from the milkweeds it eats. Monarchs migrate, sometimes hundreds of miles, each year. During migrations they can sometimes be found by the thousands clustered in a single glade or even in people's yards.

WHERE TO FIND In North America, the monarch butterfly can be found year-round in Florida and Arizona, but ranges from southern Canada to northern South America, Bermuda and the Caribbean, and Hawaii and islands throughout the Pacific.

Giant Silk Moth
(Antheraea polyphemus)

DOMAIN: EUKARYOTA
KINGDOM: ANIMALIA
PHYLUM: ARTHROPODA
CLASS: INSECTA
ORDER: LEPIDOPTERA
FAMILY: SATURNIIDAE
GENUS: *Antheraea*
SPECIES: *A. polyphemus*

This moth's tan or reddish-brown colors help camouflage it among tree bark and leaves. Patches of color on its hind wings look like the eyes of an owl. Scientists believe these eyespots scare away predators. The moth can be startling to a human, too—it has a 7-inch wingspan. The imago (or adult form) of this moth lives only about a week; its adult life is spent seeking mates and, in the case of the female, laying eggs. The male finds the female by smelling special chemicals she emits, called pheromones. He smells with his feathery antennae, which are noticeably bigger and shaggier than the female's. The caterpillar of the giant silk moth often folds itself into a leaf to make its cocoon.

WHERE TO FIND You can find giant silk moths in North America, from northern Mexico through Canada.

Luna Moth
(Actias luna)

DOMAIN: EUKARYOTA
KINGDOM: ANIMALIA
PHYLUM: ARTHROPODA
CLASS: INSECTA
ORDER: LEPIDOPTERA
FAMILY: SATURNIIDAE
GENUS: *Actias*
SPECIES: *A. luna*

Like the giant silk moth, this pale green moth has eyespots on its wings to startle and deter predators. As a caterpillar, the luna moth deters predators with a different technique—a clicking noise. If a predator ignores this warning, the caterpillar discourages it further by vomiting. Even in its cocoon, the pupa can still make the warning noise and thrash around. Like giant silk moths, lunas live as adults for only about a week. They have already done all their eating as caterpillars; their imago form doesn't even have a mouth.

WHERE TO FIND The Luna moth is found in the eastern regions of North America, from northern Mexico through Canada.

Evergreen Bagworm Moth COCOON

(Thyridopteryx ephemeraeformis)

DOMAIN: EUKARYOTA
KINGDOM: ANIMALIA
PHYLUM: ARTHROPODA
CLASS: INSECTA
ORDER: LEPIDOPTERA
FAMILY: PSYCHIDAE
GENUS: *Thyridopteryx*
SPECIES: *T. ephemeraeformis*

An evergreen bagworm's cocoon is often found on cedar trees. A cedar stays green all year long. Its leaves are needles, somewhat like those found on a pine tree. The moth cocoon is covered with these needles so thoroughly that it appears to be part of the tree. The cocoon is hidden inside a "bag" made out of silk and bits of the tree, so you might mistake it for a pinecone. It's such a clever disguise that most predators don't eat the bagworm because they don't realize it's there. The cocoon itself is about the length of your finger and as thick as a pencil, and it's pointy on both ends.

A person can pick the cocoon from the tree like a fruit, but it's tough to tear open. If you do open one, you'll find a black caterpillar inside. Like most animals that live in the dark, it will dislike the light. It will writhe and pull itself further inside the cocoon.

Late in the summer, it becomes easier to see that the cocoons are not part of the tree. The needles woven into the bags die and turn brown or rusty colored, while the needles on the trees stay green.

Most moths only live in a cocoon while they are pupae. A bagworm is different: It spends almost its whole life in its cocoon. It can stick its head out of the cocoon to eat needles or other leaves. It can stick its legs out to crawl to new food or climb a tree. It can raise and lower itself on its silk threads. At the back end of the cocoon is a hole for its waste to drop through. (By the way, insects don't have separate feces and urine. Their waste comes out mixed together.)

A male bagworm grows up to look very strange. It is a moth, but it looks more like a bee. Its wings are clear like a bee's. Its body is very hairy. It doesn't live long—only between two and seven days. It can't even eat. It did all of its eating when it was a caterpillar. It flies around until it finds a female to mate with. Then it dies.

The female doesn't even come out of her cocoon. She never grows wings or flies. She waits inside the cocoon for a male to come and mate with her. She lets the male know where she is by giving off a strong smell. Most female insects lay eggs after mating. Not the bagworm! She just dies with the eggs still inside her. The eggs are well protected: They're inside her body, which is inside her cocoon.

When the eggs hatch, the little larvae crawl out of her body and then out of the cocoon. They lower themselves on threads of silk. Sometimes the wind blows them away to other trees. Wherever they land, they start their new lives. They begin by making a cocoon. At first they are too little to bite off bits of the tree for their cocoons. So they use their own waste and some silk. As they get bigger, they add bits of leaves and such.

WHERE TO FIND In the US, the evergreen bagworm is found from Massachusetts south to Florida and west to Nebraska and Colorado. Similar species occur in most of North and South America and in the southern reaches of Canada. Since these moths are plentiful and sometimes harmful to the trees they live on, there's no reason not to take them in the wild.

HOW TO PIN A MOTH OR BUTTERFLY

Once you've collected a butterfly or moth, pinning it is the best way to preserve it. If the insect has been dead for more than a few hours, it will probably be stiff. You won't be able to change its pose. However, if it is still fresh and flexible, you can flatten the wings out to show them to their best advantage. To do this, you will need a setting board (sometimes called a spreading board). A setting board is a simple device. It has a gutter between two raised flat sections. The gutter is for the body of the butterfly. The flat sections hold the wings up. You can make this gadget yourself with cardboard and balsa wood or Styrofoam.

WHAT YOU NEED:

- One 4" x 6" piece of cardboard or basswood
- One ¼" x 2 ½" x 6" pieces of balsa wood
- At least four to six pieces of card stock
- Glue
- Pins

1. Apply glue to the back of the two pieces of balsa wood.

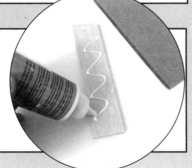

2. Attach the pieces of wood to the cardboard. Leave about ¾" gutter between the two pieces of wood.

3. Pin your butterfly directly into the gutter. Gently spread its wings wide, letting them rest on top of the strips of balsa wood. Place the thin strips of card stock over the wings to hold them in place, and pin them at the ends. You may need four to six strips to hold the wings firmly.

4. Let the butterfly sit for twenty-four hours. After that, it will be stiff. You won't be able to change its position again without breaking the wings. Remove it from the setting board and pin it wherever you like (maybe in the cabinet you made yourself!).

If the insect has been dead for a while, it will be too stiff to position. In that case, you can simply pin it through its thorax (the section of the body that comes between the head and the abdomen). You can pin it onto a flat piece of cardboard or directly into your cabinet. As you push the pin in, be careful not to drive it through any wings or legs. Leave part of the pin sticking out above and below the body.

Pinning makes an insect easy to look at. If you want to examine the underside, you just pull the pin out and turn the insect over.

FLIES and MOSQUITOS

Most insects have four wings. What distinguishes the "true flies" (order Diptera) is having only two wings. Instead of hind wings, they have tiny stubs called halteres, which they use for balance in flying. Their larvae have no legs. Some of them simply look like worms; these are called maggots. Other fly larvae have a distinct, hard head. Certain flies perform the most impressive aerial feats of any animal. For example, some species flap their wings more than one thousand times per second—the highest rate in the animal kingdom. A number of species can fly backward as well as forward and even land on ceilings.

Common Housefly
(*Musca domestica*)

DOMAIN: EUKARYOTA
KINGDOM: ANIMALIA
PHYLUM: ARTHROPODA
CLASS: INSECTA
ORDER: DIPTERA
FAMILY: MUSCIDAE
GENUS: *Musca*
SPECIES: *M. domestica*

Houseflies are the kind you mostly see buzzing around your home on a summer day. They can be pests, but they are also very interesting animals.

For example, a housefly knows how to partly digest its meals before it eats them. To do this, it spits some of its digestive juice onto the food. The juice has an acid that breaks the food down into a liquid. The fly sucks down this liquid. Really, a fly doesn't eat; it just drinks. This is one reason people don't want flies in their houses. The fly may spit on their food. Sometimes a fly even lands on a person and drinks some of his or her sweat.

Flies will eat almost anything a person eats, plus many other things we wouldn't think of as food. A fly's very favorite food is bird waste. (Remember how insects don't have separate urine and feces? The same is true of most birds.) A housefly especially likes to hang around chicken coops, where there is lots of bird waste.

Another interesting thing about the housefly is its big eyes. Each of its eyes can see in nearly every direction at once. That's why it's hard to sneak up on a fly.

WHERE TO FIND For a cabinet keeper, the best thing about houseflies is that they are easy to find. Look for them near windows. Often, a fly moves toward the window because it's attracted to sunlight. It doesn't understand windows. It will bump its head on the window over and over as it tries to get to the light. Like most insects, flies have simple brains and aren't good at figuring out new situations. Sometimes a fly will stay near the window until the sunlight dries it out and it dies.

HOW TO COLLECT To collect a housefly, you can pin it through the thorax, just as you would a butterfly. Handle them with gloves, because they may have harmful germs on them.

Bottle Fly
(family Calliphoridae)

DOMAIN: EUKARYOTA
KINGDOM: ANIMALIA
PHYLUM: ARTHROPODA
CLASS: INSECTA
ORDER: DIPTERA
FAMILY: CALLIPHORIDAE

Bottle flies are some of the most beautiful insects you will ever see, but also the grossest. First, the beautiful part: their color. They look like houseflies made of shiny metal. Some of them are green, some blue. Some are even gold.

Now, the gross part: They eat dead things. The mother fly lays her eggs in a dead animal, or carcass. The fly larva hatch out and eat the meat of the carcass. They live in the carcass, eating, until they are ready to become pupae. The most amazing thing about bottle flies is how they find a carcass. Some of them can smell a carcass from ten miles away!

That keen sense of smell can be fooled, however. We've already discussed animals that mimic the appearance of others. There are also flowers that mimic the smell of dead animals. Their rotten smell allows them to attract bottle flies and other carrion-eating insects. The bottle flies land on the flowers and sip their nectar. The benefit for the plant is pollination: The fly spreads its pollen to other flowers, which is the plant's way of mating.

WHERE TO FIND There are various species of bottle flies, including the green bottle fly and the blue bottle fly. Green bottle flies prefer temperate and tropical regions—mainly in the Southern Hemisphere. Blue bottles and other bottle flies are found in most areas of the Western Hemisphere.

Mosquito
(family Culicidae)

DOMAIN: EUKARYOTA
KINGDOM: ANIMALIA
PHYLUM: ARTHROPODA
CLASS: INSECTA
ORDER: DIPTERA
FAMILY: CULICIDAE

Mosquitos are flies with an interesting life cycle. The mother mosquito lays her eggs on water. The larvae live in the water. They eat living things they find floating there—bacteria, tiny plants, stuff like that. They float with their heads downward. They breathe through tubes that come out of their rear ends.

After its pupa stage, the imago mosquito flies around feeding on plant juices. The males never bite animals at all. The females only drink from people or other animals when they are about to lay eggs. Blood has extra protein that helps the females make the eggs. How can you tell the males from the females? For one thing, only the males buzz. You can't hear the females unless they bump against your ear. For another thing, males have fuzzy antennae. There are hundreds of species of mosquitoes, and not all of them bite people.

WHERE TO FIND Mosquitos are found in every part of the world, with the exception of Antarctica and Iceland.

HOW TO COLLECT Mosquitoes are difficult to collect because their bodies break easily. The best way to mount them is called pointing. To point an insect, you first cut out a small triangle of stiff paper, such as card stock. It's best to use white paper so that the insect will show up well. Put a single dot of glue on one tip of the triangle. Now touch the glue dot against the insect's belly so that the insect sticks. Let it dry. Now, simply put a pin through the paper and stick it onto a piece of cardboard or foam with your other insects.

BEETLES

A fully grown beetle, like most insects, has four wings. The wings in front are hard. They fold over the beetle's back, making a kind of shell, which protects the hind wings and the abdomen. These front wings are called elytra. (The singular is elytron.) They can be almost any color. On ladybug beetles, they are usually orange or red with black spots. On June beetles, they can be gold, bright green, or brown.

The hind wings are usually clear, like the wings of a housefly or a honeybee. They lie folded under the elytra until the beetle wants to fly. Then the elytra stick up out of the way and the hind wings unfold. They do most of the work of flying.

There are about 400,000 kinds of beetles. In fact, there are more kinds of beetles than of any other group of insects. That means you will never run out of beetles to find. Beetles work well in cabinets because of their hard elytra. The exoskeleton on other parts of their bodies, such as the head, also tends to be hard. They last a long time.

Here are some interesting features you may find on different beetles:

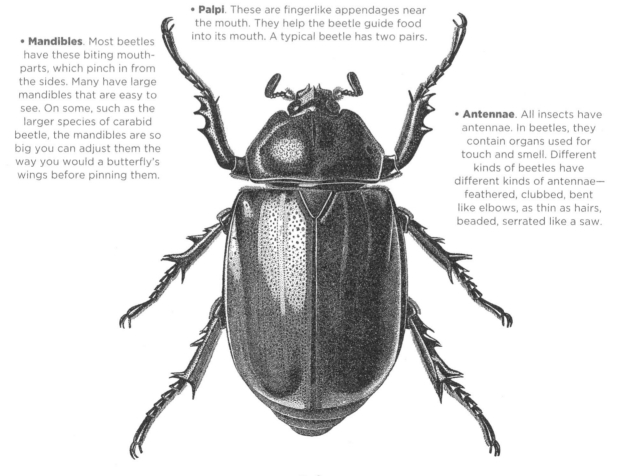

• **Palpi**. These are fingerlike appendages near the mouth. They help the beetle guide food into its mouth. A typical beetle has two pairs.

• **Mandibles**. Most beetles have these biting mouthparts, which pinch in from the sides. Many have large mandibles that are easy to see. On some, such as the larger species of carabid beetle, the mandibles are so big you can adjust them the way you would a butterfly's wings before pinning them.

• **Antennae**. All insects have antennae. In beetles, they contain organs used for touch and smell. Different kinds of beetles have different kinds of antennae—feathered, clubbed, bent like elbows, as thin as hairs, beaded, serrated like a saw.

Jewel Beetles (family Buprestidae)

DOMAIN: EUKARYOTA
KINGDOM: ANIMAL
PHYLUM: ARTHROPODA
CLASS: INSECTA
ORDER: COLEOPTERA
FAMILY: BUPRESTIDAE

Jewel beetles are boring. I don't mean they're uninteresting—I mean they literally bore holes as they eat their way through leaves, roots, stems, and even the trunks of trees. What makes them interesting are their iridescent colors. They shine because the outer layers of their exoskeletons are partially transparent. That causes the colors of the beetle to change when you look at it from different angles. They also change according to how bright the light is. Jewel beetles can be picky about the plants they eat. One species prefers pine trees damaged by forest fires. It can smell pine smoke fifty miles away and can literally see heat.

WHERE TO FIND Jewel beetles are found all over the world, but the most colorful are in India, Thailand, Japan, and other parts of Asia.

Cyphogastra javanica

Catoxantha opulenta

Chrysochroa buqueti

Polybothris sumptuosa gema

Cyphogastra javanica

Anthaxia passerini

Sphenoptera rauca

Lamprodila rutilans

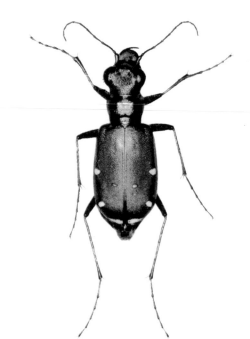

Six-Spotted
Tiger Beetle

(Cicindela sexguttata)

DOMAIN: EUKARYOTA
KINGDOM: ANIMALIA
PHYLUM: ARTHROPODA
CLASS: INSECTA
ORDER: COLEOPTERA
FAMILY: CARABIDAE
GENUS: *Cicindela*
SPECIES: *C. sexguttata*

Sometimes it can be hard to find the eyes on an insect. Some insects don't even have eyes! But it's easy to find the bulging eyes of the six-spotted tiger beetle. The rest of its face is small and pointed. It looks like an alien from a movie.

This beetle is about the size of a housefly. It's green, and so shiny it looks like it's made of metal. It has six white spots scattered on its elytra.

Why is this beetle called a "tiger"? Because it's a dangerous predator to other bugs. (Not to people, though.) It runs along the ground at amazing speeds. It grabs other bugs and bites them to death. Then it eats them. Often, it leaves nothing but the legs.

You have to be quick to catch a tiger beetle. When you get close to one, it flies away. Even if it is facing you, it can just fly away backward. Those bulging eyes give it a big advantage. Like a housefly, it can see danger coming from any direction.

WHERE TO FIND Six-spotted tiger beetles can be found in forested regions from the central US to the East Coast, and as far north as Ontario, Canada, and as far south as Kentucky.

THERE ARE MORE THAN FOUR THOUSAND SPECIES OF FLOWER CHAFER BEETLES.

Protaetia affinis

Protaetia cuprea

Flower Chafer

(family Scarabaeidae)

DOMAIN: EUKARYOTA
KINGDOM: ANIMALIA
PHYLUM: ARTHROPODA
CLASS: INSECTA
ORDER: COLEOPTERA
FAMILY: SCARABAEIDAE

Flower chafers are members of the subfamily Cetoniinae in the family Scarabaeida. Most of them feed on the nectar of flowers or on fruit, though a few prey on other insects. What sets the flower chafers apart is the huge variety of colors found in different species. One species has white spots on a dark brown background, so it looks something like a domino. Another has a tigerlike pattern of orange stripes on a black background. A third is blotched with orange, yellow, and black, as if it were made of lava. Another is red on its head and the forward part of its thorax (the prothorax), but its wings come in an array of metallic colors—green, blue, gold. There are more than four thousand species, and hundreds of them are colorful and collectible. The ones pictured above are *Protaetia affinis*, which comes in gleaming shades of green or gold, and *P. cuprea,* which can be gold, bronze, green, and rose.

WHERE TO FIND Flower chafers are most commonly found in southern and central Europe.

Rainbow Scarab Dung Beetle

(Phanaeus demon)

DOMAIN: EUKARYOTA
KINGDOM: ANIMALIA
PHYLUM: ARTHROPODA
CLASS: INSECTA
ORDER: COLEOPTERA
FAMILY: SCARABAEIDAE
GENUS: *Phanaeus*
SPECIES: *P. demon*

Nothing gets wasted in nature—not even feces. Thousands of beetles in different families specialize in eating it, especially the feces of herbivores like cattle and elephants. These beetles follow one of three different patterns for processing the dung. Telecoprids roll it along the ground to form it into balls, sometimes much bigger than themselves, and then they lay eggs in the balls. The larvae then hatch and eat the ball from within. Endocoprids simply find a pile of dung and live inside it themselves, as well as lay eggs in it. Paracoprids tunnel beneath the dung. They pull bits of the dung into the tunnels and form it into balls onto which they lay their eggs. Most dung beetles have interesting shapes—for example, special combs on their feet for handling dung, or horns on their heads. Some of the most beautiful are found in the genus *Phanaeus*. For example, *Phanaeus demon* (pictured) has a brilliant, metallic green color. The rainbow scarab, *Phanaeus vindex*, can come in various colors; the most attractive are combinations of red, green, and bronze, all with a metallic luster.

WHERE TO FIND Rainbow scarab dung beetles are found in the eastern US and as far west as Colorado.

Predaceous Diving Beetle

(family Dytiscidae)

DOMAIN: EUKARYOTA
KINGDOM: ANIMALIA
PHYLUM: ARTHROPODA
CLASS: INSECTA
ORDER: COLEOPTERA
FAMILY: DYTISCIDAE

"Predaceous" means a predator. It lives by eating other animals. This big diving beetle can eat other bugs, plus tadpoles and small fish. Its larva, which is found in ponds and creeks, is called a water tiger. It's long and snaky, but with legs like a grown-up beetle. It uses its massive jaws to grab other animals swimming in the water.

When the larva grows up into a beetle, it still lives in water. It can get big for an insect—more than an inch and half long. It is smooth and shaped to glide through water. It makes itself even smoother by folding its front and middle legs under its thorax, pointing forward. It folds its hind legs under its abdomen, pointing backward. From above, you can't see the legs at all. The beetle looks like a dark brown teardrop. This is its shape in life, and also in death. If you see one at a pond, you may have to poke it with a stick to make sure it's dead.

Like lots of beetles that live in water, the predaceous diving beetle has wide hind legs to help it swim. They are attached at about the middle of its body. When it swims, it uses those legs like the paddles in a rowboat. They kick like crazy. The beetle goes zooming around the pond.

WHERE TO FIND These aquatic beetles can be found in lakes, rock pools, and watery environments throughout the world.

Ladybug
(family Coccinellidae)

DOMAIN: EUKARYOTA
KINGDOM: ANIMALIA
PHYLUM: ARTHROPODA
CLASS: INSECTA
ORDER: COLEOPTERA
FAMILY: COCCINELLIDAE

Ladybugs—sometimes called lady-birds—aren't true bugs or birds, but beetles. The family Coccinellidae is large, containing more than five thousand species. Most of them have elytra with black spots on a background of red, orange, or yellow. The rest of the body is typically black with white spots. Their shape is rounded like a drop of water. It's a durable shape, making them hard to crush. It also makes it hard for ants and other predators to get a hold of them.

Many ladybugs are themselves predators; they feed on tiny arthropods such as aphids, scale insects, and mites. Those arthropods often feed on food plants and fruit trees, so ladybugs are generally welcome in gardens and orchards. However, problems have happened when people tried to import extra ladybugs to control the aphids. For example, an Asian species called the harlequin ladybug was imported to the US in 1916. The imports ate plenty of aphids, but, unlike the native species, they weren't content to cluster in trees to survive the winter. Instead, they invaded houses. In places like Minnesota and Wisconsin, they are often found indoors even in the coldest part of winter, clinking against lightbulbs in their flight and even crawling on people in their sleep.

A ladybug's orange and black colors are similar to those of the monarch butterfly, and they advertise the same thing: bad taste. Not only does a ladybug taste bad, but it secretes a foul-smelling fluid from glands on its knees to deter predators. You can let a ladybug crawl on your hand without worrying about the smell—just remember not to pinch it.

WHERE TO FIND There are over five thousand species of ladybugs all over the world. In the US, they can be found in fields, forests, parks, gardens, and yards in the summertime. Sometimes, after a cold spell, they will swarm onto a building illuminated by the sun—most typically this happens in the early fall (depending on the location and weather conditions).

THERE ARE SEVERAL MYTHS ABOUT LADYBUGS. ONE IS THAT THEY BRING GOOD LUCK—OR BAD LUCK TO THE PERSON WHO KILLS ONE. ANOTHER MYTH IS THAT YOU CAN TELL THE AGE OF A LADYBUG ACCORDING TO HOW MANY SPOTS IT HAS. NOT TRUE. THE NUMBER OF SPOTS ON A LADYBUG HAS TO DO WITH WHAT SPECIES IT BELONGS TO. THERE ARE MORE THAN FIVE THOUSAND SPECIES IN THE WORLD!

LADYBUGS ARE ALSO KNOWN AS LADYBIRDS. THERE'S A FAVORITE OLD NURSERY RHYME FOR CHILDREN: LADYBIRD, LADYBIRD, FLY AWAY HOME; YOUR HOUSE IS ON FIRE, YOUR CHILDREN ARE GONE; ALL EXCEPT ONE, AND THAT'S LITTLE ANN, FOR SHE HAS CREPT UNDER THE WARMING PAN.

Hercules Rhinoceros Beetle
(*Dynastes hercules*)

DOMAIN: EUKARYOTA
KINGDOM: ANIMALIA
PHYLUM: ARTHROPODA
CLASS: INSECTA
ORDER: COLEOPTERA
FAMILY: SCARABAEIDAE
GENUS: *Dynastes*
SPECIES: *D. hercules*

Rhinoceros beetles make up the subfamily Dynastinae. They're called rhinoceros beetles because the males generally have horns—one curving up from the head and one jutting forward from the thorax. These beetles have thick, durable exoskeletons. Some of them are among the largest insects known. One of those giants is the Hercules beetle. The biggest males of this species reach 6¾ inches long. A lot of that is horn. Only two other beetles reach similar size. Despite the size, though, the beetle is harmless to us. Its mouthparts aren't made for biting.

Even as a wormy-looking, black-headed larva, the Hercules beetle is huge. It's thick and can reach 4½ inches. When harassed, it curls into the shape of a letter *C*. In this position, it's big enough to fill a man's hand. It spends its time eating rotting wood. As an adult, it's more interested in fallen fruit. The male's lower horn looks a bit like a deer's branched antler. The upper one looks something like a hairbrush, with rusty fibers projecting from its underside.

WHERE TO FIND Rhinoceros beetles can be found in the tropical rain forests of South and Central America, as well as some islands in the Caribbean.

RHINOCEROS BEETLES ARE AMONG THE STRONGEST ANIMALS IN THE WORLD! AN ADULT RHINO BEETLE CAN LIFT OVER EIGHT HUNDRED TIMES ITS BODY WEIGHT. THAT WOULD BE LIKE AN AVERAGE MAN BEING ABLE TO LIFT FORTY CARS AT ONCE.

HOW TO PRESERVE A BEETLE

When you collect a beetle, pinning is usually the easiest way to preserve it. Push the pin right through its thorax. If the thorax is too hard, you can put the pin through the abdomen, right behind the thorax and between the wings. Putting a pin in this spot will sometimes make the wings spread open. You might choose that spot on purpose just to show what the wings look like. Or, you can leave the wings folded to show off the elytra.

When you pin it, you may accidentally break the hard exoskeleton on the thorax. This isn't really a problem. Beetles often accidentally break this part themselves. For example, June beetles buzz around porch lights, and they are likely to bash into a building and injure themselves. They don't seem to mind

having a few cracks in their exoskeletons. They just keep going. Sometimes, while pinning a beetle, you may also accidentally knock off a leg or two. That's easy to do if your beetle has been dead for more than a day or two. Don't worry about it. If I really want to have a complete specimen, I just glue the leg back on.

You can also just keep your beetle in a clear plastic bag inside your cabinet. This is a good choice if you want to take it out and handle it. The bag allows you to look at your beetle from top and underneath. The more you handle it, the more legs and antennae will fall off. Other than that, beetles can get handled a lot and still hold up. In this way, they're more fun to collect than most other insects.

GRASSHOPPERS and LOCUSTS

Grasshoppers are insects with powerful hind legs built for jumping, and relatively short antennae. They undergo an incomplete metamorphosis, with the nymph looking much like a wingless adult. They are sometimes called "short-horned" grasshoppers to distinguish them from similar looking insects called katydids. Because they depend on camouflage as protection from predators, grasshoppers come in a variety of colors to hide them among different kinds of plants. Some look like rough gray bark; some are a pale mint-green; some are speckled with red to match the autumn foliage. The biggest are longer than a soda can. On a big grasshopper, it's easy to see features like its many mouthparts and five eyes. So far, scientists have cataloged more than eleven thousand species.

About a dozen of those species, not closely related to each other, are capable of becoming locusts. When their population explodes and outstrips their food supply, these special grasshoppers change color and grow into a larger, stronger adult form. They are still recognizable as grasshoppers, but they are now capable of flying long distances in swarms. They do so in order to find more food.

Short-horned grasshoppers are closely related to crickets and katydids (see pages 94–95). Sometimes, they can be hard to tell apart. Some of the traits listed here don't always hold true, but most of the time they will help you to categorize a particular insect.

Grasshoppers including Locusts
- short antennae
- make noise by rubbing hind legs against the forewing
- active during the day
- herbivorous

Crickets and Katydids
- long antennae
- make noise by rubbing forewings together
- active during the night
- sometimes omnivorous

Red-Legged Grasshopper (*Melanoplus femurrubrum*)

DOMAIN: EUKARYOTA
KINGDOM: ANIMALIA
PHYLUM: ARTHROPODA
CLASS: INSECTA
ORDER: ORTHOPTERA
FAMILY: ACRIDIDAE
GENUS: *Melanoplus*
SPECIES: *M. femurrubrum*

This species is common in the US, Canada, and Mexico. It is usually patterned with green, yellow, and black, although an occasional specimen has flashy patches of blue or orange. What makes it fairly distinct is the red on its big hind legs. It eats hundreds of different kinds of plants. Like many grasshoppers, this species survives the winter by laying its eggs in soil. The adults die with the coming of the frost, but the eggs hatch in the spring to start a new generation.

WHERE TO FIND **This species of grasshopper can be found throughout North America.**

Desert Locust (*Schistocerca gregaria*)

DOMAIN: EUKARYOTA
KINGDOM: ANIMALIA
PHYLUM: ARTHROPODA
CLASS: INSECTA
ORDER: ORTHOPTERA
FAMILY: ACRIDIDAE
GENUS: *Schistocerca*
SPECIES: *S. gregaria*

Locusts are famous for eating. Sometimes they eat as much food in a day as their weight. In parts of Africa, the Middle East, and Asia, billions of desert locusts form swarms that eat every scrap of plant life for miles in every direction. Such a swarm can cause a famine. In some years, one out of every ten people on earth is affected by food shortages caused by these locusts. Their swarming can even create a kind of smog, as the locusts jostle each other in flight and fill the air with feces and bits of exoskeleton.

WHERE TO FIND **Desert locusts can be found in Africa, the Middle East, and Asia.**

KATYDIDS and CRICKETS

Katydids look similar to grasshoppers because their hind legs are much bigger than their front and middle legs. In fact, katydids are sometimes called "long-horned grasshoppers." They don't really have horns, just antennae. The antennae can be longer than the rest of the katydid's body.

Another trait you may notice about katydids is their long ovipositors. An ovipositor is a special tool for laying eggs. It sticks out of the back of some insects. The most well-known ovipositors are the stingers on wasps and bees. But those are only famous for stinging. Most people don't even know they are also used for laying eggs. A katydid has two long ovipositors. They look like a pair of swords sticking out of its back end.

Many katydids have wings that come together over their backs in a ridge, like the roof of a house. But some katydids don't have wings at all. They just walk.

Katydids are named for the sound some of them make. They make the sound by rubbing their legs across a special membrane of their wings. One common kind of katydid is bright green. It looks like a leaf. In fact, katydids can use their color as camouflage when hiding in trees.

HOW TO COLLECT A GRASSHOPPER OR KATYDID

The trouble with collecting big grasshoppers is that they have fleshy abdomens. The liquids inside their abdomens won't simply dry up, as sometimes happens with smaller specimens. Instead, it may rot and leak out, creating a foul-smelling mess. There's a special trick for pinning such fleshy insects. It's called evisceration. It means draining the liquid so it doesn't make a mess later. I suggest you do this carefully, as it involves the use of sharp instruments. Children should get the help of an adult.

1. First, just pin the insect as usual. Remember, you want the pin to go through the middle section of its body—the thorax. This part is hard in most insects, even if they have squishy parts elsewhere.

2. Now, you'll need a small, sharp blade. A paring knife used for peeling apples is fine. Make a small cut on the squishy back section of the insect—the abdomen. The cut should go along the side of the abdomen, where people won't be able to see it. You want to cut through the insect's hard outer layer, but no deeper than that.

3. Next, the innards have to come out. If you're lucky, they'll dribble out like spilled water. Otherwise, you have to take them out. The best way to do this is with a small syringe. Use it to gently suck the liquid out of the body.

IF YOU DON'T WANT TO MESS WITH EVISCERATION, YOU CAN ALSO PRESERVE A SQUISHY INSECT IN A VIAL FILLED WITH RUBBING ALCOHOL. THE ALCOHOL KILLS GERMS, SO THE INSECT WON'T ROT FOR A LONG TIME. SOMETIMES ALCOHOL CAUSES BRIGHT COLORS TO FADE, SO IT'S NOT A GOOD METHOD FOR BUTTERFLIES. THE ALCOHOL GIVES OFF FUMES AND CAN STING YOUR EYES, SO USE IT CAREFULLY.

Field Cricket (family Gryllidae)

DOMAIN: EUKARYOTA
KINGDOM: ANIMALIA
PHYLUM: ARTHROPODA
CLASS: INSECTA
ORDER: ORTHOPTERA
FAMILY: GRYLLIDAE

Field crickets are best known for their chirping sound. Only the males chirp; they do it to attract females. The female can tell a lot about the male from his chirp. Besides his location, it also tells her how healthy and well-fed he is. She chooses the healthiest male she can hear. Even if it's not chirping, you can tell the gender of a cricket by whether or not you see a long ovipositor on its hind end. Both sexes have several pairs of sensory organs jutting out behind them, but only the female has a single long, clubbed ovipositor.

WHERE TO FIND Field crickets can be found in fields and grasslands in warmer climates all around the world.

Mormon Cricket (*Anabrus simplex*)

DOMAIN: EUKARYOTA
KINGDOM: ANIMALIA
PHYLUM: ARTHROPODA
CLASS: INSECTA
ORDER: ORTHOPTERA
FAMILY: TETTIGONIIDAE
GENUS: *Anabrus*
SPECIES: *A. simplex*

Even though it's called a cricket, this insect is really a katydid. It is very big, sometimes 3 inches long. Mormon crickets normally eat plants and other insects. Some years the Mormon crickets swarm by the millions, eating everything in sight. Unlike swarming grasshoppers, they have no wings, so their swarms move simply by walking—sometimes more than a mile a day. As they march, they eat not only any plants in their path, but also dead animals, such as skunks run over by cars. In one case, scientists reported them eating a rattlesnake; no one knows whether the insects killed the snake or found it dead. Mormon crickets that walk too slowly get trampled and eaten by the others. Sometimes the marching swarm is so thick that it endangers people in cars—the cars crush the insects and have trouble staying on the gut-slick road.

WHERE TO FIND Mormon crickets can be found in fields and grasslands throughout western North America. A good place to look for them is near sunflowers, which they love.

Conehead Katydid (subfamily Copiphorinae)

DOMAIN: EUKARYOTA
KINGDOM: ANIMALIA
PHYLUM: ARTHROPODA
CLASS: INSECTA
ORDER: ORTHOPTERA
FAMILY: TETTIGONIIDAE
SUBFAMILY: COPIPHORINAE

This insect usually looks pretty normal for a katydid: thin legs, long, slender antennae, long ovipositors. What sets it apart is its pointy head. Having a pointy head helps it look less like an insect to predators. The cone looks sharp, like a thorn or the stem of a leaf. Since they are camouflaged to blend in with plants, coneheads are usually green or brown. But the cone itself may be a completely different color—blue, yellow, black, even orange. Sometimes the cone makes a conehead look like it's wearing a clown hat.

WHERE TO FIND Coneheads can be found along the eastern US, as far west as Texas.

DRAGONFLIES and DAMSELFLIES

A dragonfly has a long, thin body, big eyes, and four clear wings. It is usually found near water. You may see them flying over lakes, rivers, ponds, or even in your own backyard when the sprinkler is on. They stay near water because they eat mosquitoes, and mosquitoes spend most of their time near water. Dragonflies catch the mosquitoes in flight. They hold their legs in the shape of a basket and scoop the mosquitoes up as they buzz by. They also eat other flying insects, such as bees and houseflies.

Young dragonflies live in water. Like grasshoppers and katydids, dragonflies have an incomplete metamorphosis. So that means we can call their larvae "nymphs." But there's a more specific word for nymphs that live in water: naiads.

Dragonfly naiads have no wings. They breathe through gills in their rear ends. When they need to move very fast to get away from a predator, they push a lot of water out of their rear ends at once and go jetting away. Basically, they propel themselves with fart power. When they're not in danger, they just swim around eating animals they find in the water, such as other insects. Sometimes they even eat fish and tadpoles. But their favorite food is mosquito larvae. (Remember, mosquito larvae live in water, too.) You might say that eating mosquitoes is a lifelong habit for dragonflies.

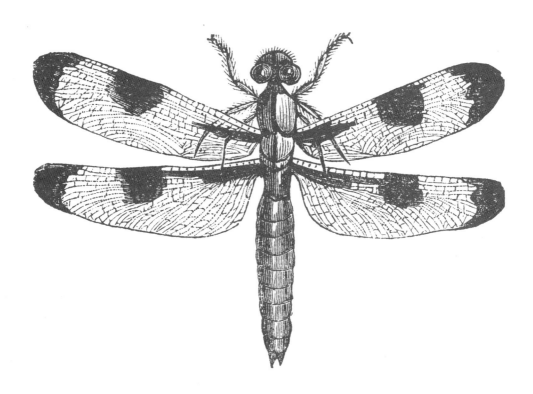

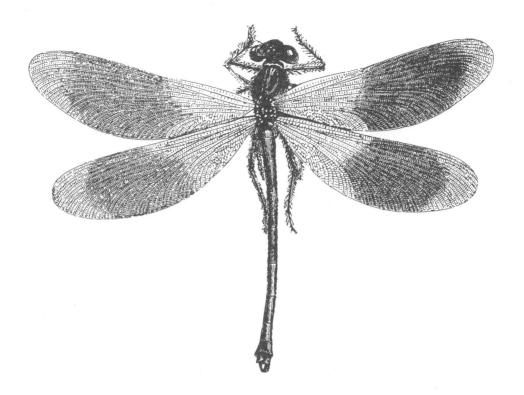

A dragonfly spends most of its life as a naiad. It can be a naiad for years, but it only lives as an imago for six to eight weeks. A dragonfly is so fast that it's hard to catch. Just like houseflies and tiger beetles, it has big eyes that allow it to see in all directions at once and make it hard to sneak up on. Their fragile bodies come in many colors—metallic blue, black, brown, green, even red.

The dragonfly has a close cousin called the damselfly. They look a lot alike. Damselflies are usually more slender than dragonflies. The way to be certain which one you're seeing is to wait until it lands. If it's a dragonfly, it will hold its wings flat and out to the sides, the same way it does when it's flying. It looks like a little airplane. If it is a damselfly, its wings will point backward instead of staying flat.

Damselflies catch insects in the air, just as dragonflies do. But they also attack bugs that are sitting around on plants.

Both dragonflies and damselflies belong to the order Odonata. Members of this ancient order have turned up in fossils at least 325 million years old—they predate the dinosaurs. How does an animal with no bones become a fossil? In the case of some ancient dragonflies, their bodies became trapped in sediment that was later compacted into limestone. The material of the insect's body is gone, but the impression remains in stone. Sometimes the impression is so precise you can see the veins in the insect's wings. Among these fossil dragonflies, some show a wingspan of 30 inches—about the same as a pigeon.

Green Darner Dragonfly (*Anax junius*)

DOMAIN: EUKARYOTA
KINGDOM: ANIMALIA
PHYLUM: ARTHROPODA
CLASS: INSECTA
ORDER: ODONATA
FAMILY: AESHNIDAE
GENUS: *Anax*
SPECIES: *A. junius*

A green darner can be more than 3 inches—about as long as a man's index finger. Its wingspan can be 4½ inches, which is wider than an average man's hand. It has bulging brown eyes. On its face is a pattern of yellow and black that looks like a target. Its thorax is green. In males, the abdomen is bright blue; in females, it's purple.

WHERE TO FIND The green darner can be found throughout North America, as well as in the Caribbean and parts of Asia.

Flame Skimmer Dragonfly (*Libellula saturata*)

DOMAIN: EUKARYOTA
KINGDOM: ANIMALIA
PHYLUM: ARTHROPODA
CLASS: INSECTA
ORDER: ODONATA
FAMILY: LIBELLULIDAE
GENUS: *Libellula*
SPECIES: *L. saturata*

This dragonfly species is named for the color of the males. Their bodies are a fiery orange. Their wings have orange patches that you can see through, like colored glass. Their eyes can be brown or a dark red. Flame skimmer dragonflies are about as long as a woman's index finger.

WHERE TO FIND Flame skimmers can be found in fields and parks throughout the southwestern US. They favor warm ponds and streams.

Ebony Jewelwing Damselfly *(Calopteryx maculata)*

DOMAIN: EUKARYOTA
KINGDOM: ANIMALIA
PHYLUM: ARTHROPODA
CLASS: INSECTA
ORDER: ODONATA
FAMILY: CALOPTERYGIDAE
GENUS: *Calopteryx*
SPECIES: *C. maculata*

The males of this species have a blue-green body that shines like metal. Their wings are like black velvet. The females have brownish bodies with wings that look like black glass. At the tips of their wings are white spots. What makes ebony jewelwings stand out is the way they fly. Most damselflies and dragonflies zoom around. They are among the fastest-flying insects. But the ebony jewelwing flutters, like a butterfly. They've been described as "bits of silk caught in a breeze."

WHERE TO FIND The ebony jewelwing can be found near streams, lakes, and rivers along the eastern US.

HOW TO PRESERVE A DRAGONFLY

To preserve a dragonfly, the best approach is pinning. They are still fragile in death, so it's easy to break them. However, they are good insects to keep in a cabinet because they contain very little fluid, which means very little mess.

1. Place your dragonfly facedown on your spreading board, which can be a piece of Styrofoam or soft board. It should have a groove in the middle large enough to accommodate the body of the dragonfly.

2. Gently place the dragonfly so the body rests snugly in the groove.

3. Pierce the dragonfly with your insect pin in the middle through the back between the front set of wings.

4. Pin the tail of the dragonfly so it doesn't swivel.

5. The wings of the dragonfly should be flush against the spreading board. If need be, use wax strips and bracing pins to nudge the wings into the right position, and allow to dry for a few days. Then, remove bracing pins and wax paper. Unpin your specimen from the spreading board and place it in your cabinet of curiosities.

PHASMIDS and MANTISES

Insects are always looking for ways to escape from predators. Some fly fast, like the six-spotted tiger beetle. Some taste bad, so nothing will want to eat them, like the monarch butterfly. Some of them, like bagworms and coneheads, use camouflage. Another group of insects that uses camouflage is the phasmids. Some of them look like leaves. Others look like twigs. The twiglike phasmids are called "walking sticks" or "stick insects."

Stick insects are not very good at running away. They're too slow. Instead, they are good at standing still. The more still they are, the more they look like part of the tree or bush they're on.

Phasmids know some elaborate tricks for camouflage. One type of phasmid lays eggs that look like seeds. Certain ants like to eat seeds, so they gather up the eggs and take them into their nest. The phasmid egg is safe inside the ant nest. No predators can get at it. But what about the ants? They eat the part of the egg that looks good. That part doesn't have the young phasmid in it. The ants don't care about the part that does hold the young phasmid. They just leave it lying around in their nest. Soon, the phasmid nymph hatches out. It looks like a little ant. The real ants feed it and take care of it. One day the little phasmid sneaks out of the nest and climbs up a plant stem. Now it can live as a phasmid. The ants never know they've nurtured a fake.

A mantis has bulging, round eyes and hooked front legs it uses to catch other bugs. It holds those forelegs up in front of it most of the time. A mantis is a tough predator, but it is also prey. Bigger animals, like cats and birds, will eat it. Like the phasmid, the mantis hides itself with camouflage. It is the same color as the plants it lives on.

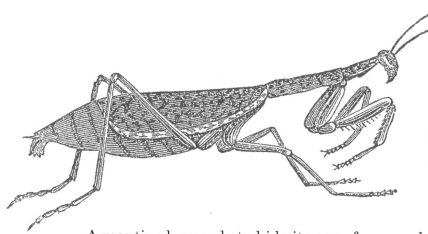

For example, it can be green like leaves. Or it can be brown like tree bark. Some are pink and white because they live on flowers that have those colors. Some can even change color to match their surroundings.

A mantis also needs to hide its eggs from predators and parasites. It hides them inside a case called an ootheca (pronounced oh-uh-THEEK-a). It looks like an army barracks—long, sort of flat, and round on top. Usually an ootheca will be stuck to a hard surface, like a tree branch or a fence. It is very hard—harder than most wood. Prying it off the surface is almost impossible. It sticks tight; it breaks before it comes loose.

How does the mantis build this ootheca? The same way people build things out of cement. To build something out of cement, you mix a special powder with water and stir it into a thick, gray liquid. Then you pour the liquid into the shape you want. The liquid hardens into cement. The mantis doesn't have a special powder, but it makes a thick liquid inside its body. Then it squeezes the liquid out of its hind end. The liquid comes out like toothpaste. The mantis shapes it by moving forward as the liquid comes out. The eggs are already in the liquid. You can't see them, but they are in two neat rows. When the liquid hits the air, it begins to harden. Soon after the mantis finishes squeezing out the liquid, it has turned into a hard ootheca. The eggs inside are safe from most predators.

The young mantises grow inside their eggs. They may hatch out in a few days. Or, if winter is coming, they may hatch when the warm weather returns.

After they hatch, each mantis nymph wants to escape. It chews a tiny hole in the ootheca. The nymphs are very pale, like snot. They are shaped like grown-up mantises. Their first job in life is to move away from the ootheca. Why? Because young mantises like to eat other young mantises. If they stay close together, many of them will fall victim to cannibalism. So each nymph goes its own way, looking for cover in grass or leaves. Because they are so small, many of them will end up getting eaten by other animals, like birds.

Now only the ootheca is left. It has two neat rows of holes along its top, made by the hatchlings. You have to look closely to see the holes. If you don't find any, the nymphs haven't hatched yet.

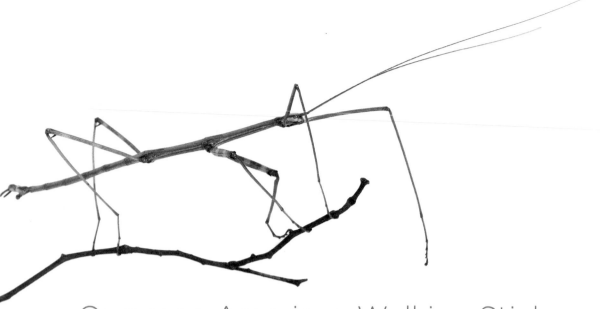

Common American Walking Stick
(*Diapheromera femorata*)

DOMAIN: EUKARYOTA
KINGDOM: ANIMALIA
PHYLUM: ARTHROPODA
CLASS: INSECTA
ORDER: PHASMATODEA
FAMILY: DIAPHEROMERIDAE
GENUS: *Diapheromera*
SPECIES: *D. femorata*

This phasmid can live on a variety of plants, but its favorites are oak and hickory trees. Its body blends in well with those trees; it looks like a branched twig. Its head and hind end even look as if they might be the buds found on a hickory twig. Its antennae are thin and long—about two thirds the length of its body. Its rear end features a pair of claspers called cerci.

WHERE TO FIND As its name suggests, this species of phasmids can be commonly found in forests and woods throughout North America.

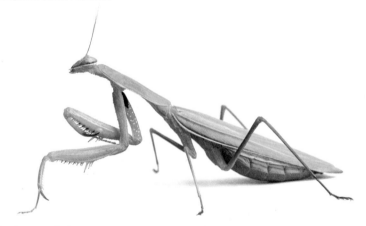

Praying Mantis (*Mantis religiosa*)

DOMAIN: EUKARYOTA
KINGDOM: ANIMALIA
PHYLUM: ARTHROPODA
CLASS: INSECTA
ORDER: MANTODEA
FAMILY: MANTIDAE
GENUS: *Mantis*
SPECIES: *M. religiosa*

Although people sometimes call any mantis a "praying mantis," this is the insect that first received that name, because its predatory pose used to give people the wrong impression. Praying mantises hunt by motion—they snag any insect they see moving. You can tell the males from the females in several ways. First, the female has a dark spot in the "armpit" beneath her front legs. Second, the male has a slender, twiglike abdomen, while the female's is thick and bulbous. Third, only males have wings. They need to fly in search of the females when it's time to mate. Sometimes the female eats the male after mating—or during.

WHERE TO FIND There are thousands of species of mantises. Regardless of the species, they can be found all over the world in temperate and tropical climates.

CICADAS

Wherever cicadas live, they are some of the biggest bugs—and the loudest. Male cicadas attract females by making noise. The male has special membranes called tymbals on his abdomen. He can make the tymbals buzz. The inside of his thick body is partly hollow, so the sound echoes inside him. Also, his throat has special chambers to create further echoes. His noise is so loud it can drown out the sound of people talking. It can go on for hours. (In general, the further south they live, the louder the cicadas.) The male sits in a tree making noise until a female joins him. After they mate, the female makes scratches in the tree bark. She lays her eggs in the scratches.

Cicadas have a complete metamorphosis. Their larvae hatch out of the tree bark and drop to the ground. Then they dig into the dirt. They live underground for a long time. Some kinds of cicada larvae stay underground for seventeen years.

When it is ready to become an adult, the larva digs a tunnel to the surface. The opening to the tunnel is as thick as a man's index finger. It's common to see dozens of these holes in the ground during the summer. After it emerges from the tunnel, the gray or brown larva crawls clumsily on the ground until it finds something it can climb, like a tree or a fence post. It climbs up a foot or two, then sheds its exoskeleton. That larval exoskeleton is a hard shell, like the chrysalis of a butterfly. It splits down the back and the adult cicada pulls itself out. At first the adult's wings are crumpled up from being inside the shell. Slowly, they straighten out. The cicada emerges with a greenish color, but as its wings straighten out, the color changes. The final color depends on the species of cicada. (There are about two thousand species.)

Dog-Day Cicada (*Tibicen canicularis*)

DOMAIN: EUKARYOTA
KINGDOM: ANIMALIA
PHYLUM: ARTHROPODA
CLASS: INSECTA
ORDER: HEMIPTERA
FAMILY: CICADIDAE
GENUS: *Tibicen*
SPECIES: *T. canicularis*

Like most cicadas, this one makes itself known during the "dog days"—the hottest part of the summer, between early July and early September. Many cicadas make a buzz, but the dog-day cicada's song is more like a mosquito's whine, except far louder. This insect looks striking, with its black body and the green veins in its transparent wings. Its larvae eat the roots of pine and oak trees.

WHERE TO FIND Dog-day cicadas can be found in the northern US, east of the Rocky Mountains and as far north as southern Canada.

BEES and WASPS

People often confuse wasps with bees—especially the yellow jacket wasp, which is yellow and black like a honeybee. However, honeybees are less aggressive than many wasps. They die when they sting a person. Wasps don't. Bees only eat pollen and nectar from flowers. Wasps eat a lot of different things, including fruit, sugary liquids, human food—and even other insects. That's why you'll find them buzzing around garbage cans and soda bottles. True bees prefer to buzz around flowers.

Some kinds of wasps are parasites. They live on another animal and eat it while it is still alive. For example, the caterpillar wasp lays its eggs on caterpillars. The wasp larvae hatch out and burrow inside the caterpillar. While the caterpillar goes around eating leaves, they eat it from inside. Finally, the wasp larvae turn into pupae. When the caterpillar dies, the wasp imagoes climb out of it and fly away.

In each colony of bees, there are three kinds of bees: queens, workers, and drones. The drones are males. Their only job is to fertilize the eggs of queens. A queen starts the colony, then mostly lays eggs. The workers are also female, but are smaller and have a different shape than the queen. They feed the larvae, forage for food, and clean and protect the hive. Worker bees can do some amazing things. For example, they dance in code to tell the other workers about food sources they've discovered. And they can raise the temperature of the hive by beating their wings rapidly.

Honeybee
(genus *Apis*)

Yellow Jacket Wasp
(genus *Vespula*)

• Bees have furry bodies.

•When flying, you can't see their legs.

• Honeybees can only sting once.
They die after stinging.

• Wasps have shiny, hairless bodies.

• When flying, you might see two thin,
long legs hanging down.

• Wasps can sting multiple times.
They do not die after stinging.

Mud Dauber Wasp (genus *Sceliphron*)

DOMAIN: EUKARYOTA
KINGDOM: ANIMALIA
PHYLUM: ARTHROPODA
CLASS: INSECTA
ORDER: HYMENOPTERA
FAMILY: SPHECIDAE
GENUS: *Sceliphron*

The mud dauber wasp builds nests of mud. It makes a little tube of mud, then it flies off to find a spider. It stings the spider to paralyze it, then carries it back to the mud tube. It puts the spider inside and lays an egg on it. It repeats this process until the whole tube is filled with spiders. When the wasp larvae hatch out, each one will have its own spider to eat.

WHERE TO FIND Different species of mud dauber wasps can be found in most parts of the world, including all of North America.

Paper Wasp (genus *Polistes*)

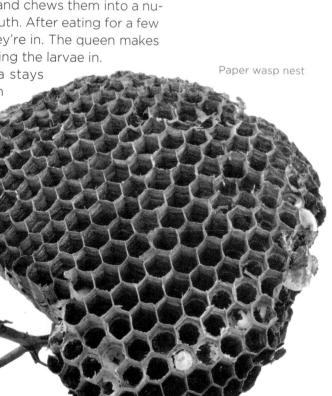

DOMAIN: EUKARYOTA
KINGDOM: ANIMALIA
PHYLUM: ARTHROPODA
CLASS: INSECTA
ORDER: HYMENOPTERA
FAMILY: VESPIDAE
GENUS: *Polistes*

This genus of wasps make paper nests. They make the paper by chewing up wood and mixing it with their saliva. (This is pretty much how people make paper, too. We grind up wood and mix it with water and certain chemicals.) The wasps spit and shape their chewed wood to make a nest. The nest usually hangs down under something, such as a branch or the eaves of a house. When a nest starts out, there is only one wasp—the queen. She makes a few tiny tubes of paper. These tubes are called cells. Each cell is like the cardboard in the middle of a roll of toilet paper. Of course, it's smaller than that—about the width of a pencil. In each cell, the queen lays an egg. The egg hatches out into a larva. Wasp larvae look like worms. They are soft and white. Their heads are hard and usually brown or red.

To feed the larvae, the queen kills other insects and chews them into a nutritious paste, which she spits right into a larva's mouth. After eating for a few days, the larvae grow so fat they fill up the cells they're in. The queen makes more paper and shapes it into lids for the cells, sealing the larvae in. Inside its cell, a larva becomes a pupa. Each pupa stays still while its body slowly changes. Its exoskeleton grows hard. Inside the exoskeleton, it changes from a wormy larva into a grown-up wasp imago. When it is done changing, it sheds its exoskeleton and chews through the lid of its cell.

Paper wasp nest

These new imagoes are workers. Workers don't mate or lay eggs. From now on, the workers will find the food and build more cells. The queen will concentrate on laying more eggs. The wasp nest gets bigger as more cells are added. Before long, it may house hundreds of wasps.

WHERE TO FIND There are hundreds of species of paper wasps that can be found all around the world.

Bumblebee (genus *Bombus*)

DOMAIN: EUKARYOTA
KINGDOM: ANIMALIA
PHYLUM: ARTHROPODA
CLASS: INSECTA
ORDER: HYMENOPTERA
FAMILY: APIDAE
GENUS: *Bombus*

Bumblebees live in colonies, usually underground. They often choose the abandoned burrows of other animals, such as rodents. The colony tends to be small—fewer than fifty members. (Compare that to honeybees, which may live in colonies of tens of thousands.) The individual bumblebee is furry. Of the more than 250 species, many have warning coloration—bright yellow or orange stripes alternating with black. Unlike monarch butterflies or ladybugs, bumblebees aren't advertising their bad taste, but their painful sting.

WHERE TO FIND Bumblebees live all over the world, with the exception of southern Africa, Australia, the Middle East, and Antarctica.

Honeybee hive

Honeybee (genus *Apis*)

DOMAIN: EUKARYOTA
KINGDOM: ANIMALIA
PHYLUM: ARTHROPODA
CLASS: INSECTA
ORDER: HYMENOPTERA
FAMILY: APIDAE
GENUS: *Apis*

Honeybees make nests much like paper wasp nests. The hollow place that holds the bee nest is called a hive. It can be a tree trunk, a cave, or a special box made by people. The cells the bees make are called a honeycomb. The honeycomb contains bee larvae and pupae. It also contains honey. Bees make honey from juices they suck out of plants. They make the honey by partly digesting the juices in their bodies. Then they spit the resulting fluid into cells. They fan their wings over the cells to evaporate most of the water contained in the fluid. The product is honey. Why do the bees make honey? It's their food. They eat it when they can't find plant juice— in the winter, mostly. Of course, people like honey, too. It's the only human food that never spoils!

WHERE TO FIND It's easy to get honeycombs from beekeepers or even from a grocery store. Keep your honeycomb in a sealed jar to protect it from other insects.

INSECT TERMS

Words relating to insects can be confusing. Partly, that's because the words come from older languages, like Latin and Greek. I am going to list the meanings of these words here in case you need them while reading.

WORD	MEANING	MORE THAN ONE IS CALLED . . .
Larva	A wormlike young insect	Larvae
Pupa	An insect that mostly stays still while it changes from a larva to an adult	Pupae
Imago	An adult insect	Imagoes
Nymph	An insect that is not fully grown. It has no wings.	Nymphs
Naiad	A nymph that lives in water	Naiads
Antenna	A feeler found on an insect's head	Antennae
Cocoon	A silk bag in which a caterpillar turns into a moth	Cocoons
Chrysalis	The hard pupa stage of a butterfly	Chrysalises or Chrysalides
Sexual dimorphism	When males and females of a species look very different	Sexual dimorphisms
Exoskeleton	The skin of an insect or other arthropod that gives it its shape	Exoskeletons
Carcass	A dead animal	Carcasses
Ootheca	The egg case of certain animals, including mantises and cockroaches	Oothecae
Thorax	The middle part of an insect's body. The legs and wings are attached to it.	Thoraxes or Thoraces
Abdomen	The back part of an insect's body. It contains the lungs and other important organs.	Abdomens
Complete metamorphosis	The shape-changing of an insect that goes through four stages in its life cycle: egg, larva, pupa, and imago	Complete metamorphoses
Incomplete metamorphosis	The shape-changing of an insect that goes through only three stages in its life cycle: egg, nymph, and imago	Incomplete metamorphoses

HOW TO AVOID GETTING STUNG

WARNING: Paper wasps can give you a painful sting. The sting can even be dangerous if you're allergic. The wasps will sting to protect their nest. So it's not a good idea to mess with wasp nests. Only collect a paper nest when you're sure the wasps won't be there. For example, in the cold of winter, wasps don't move around. They need heat. Most of them die off in cold weather. Some of them live through the winter by hibernating. If you poke a wasp when it's hibernating, it may seem dead, or it may move very slowly, like a person who is too sleepy to do much. To collect a nest in cold weather, open any cells that have lids on them and carefully discard any sleeping wasps you find inside. You may find interesting collectibles in some cells, such as dead spiders stored for food.

Even in warm weather, you may find wasp nests that have fallen down. They can get knocked down by a strong wind or a careless animal. After a few hours, wasps leave a fallen nest. They know they have to start over by building a new home. They wouldn't be safe in a nest lying on the ground. After they leave a nest behind, you can carefully collect it for your cabinet. **That said, you should always be careful approaching any nest or hive.**

ARACHNIDS
(SPIDERS, SCORPIONS, AND THEIR RELATIVES)

Spiders have eight legs. Their bodies are divided into two main parts. The front is called the cephalothorax. It has the eyes, mouth, and legs, plus some feelers called pedipalps. Sometimes the pedipalps look like extra legs, but they are shorter. The back part of the spider is called the abdomen. At the rear of the abdomen are the spinnerets, the organs the spider uses to make silk. The spinnerets look like a pair of little fingers, though they may be too small to see clearly.

Silk squirts out of the spider's body as a liquid. When it hits the air, it gets more solid. Different spiders use their silk in different ways. Here are some of the jobs silk can do for a spider:

• It can line the spider's burrow (the hole it lives in). This use is common among larger kinds, like tarantulas and wolf spiders.

• It can make a sac for the spider's eggs. The sac can be as fluffy as a cottonball or as stiff as paper.

• A baby spider (spiderling) can spin a thread of silk into the wind. The wind then carries the spiderling to some new place. This is how baby spiders separate from each other when they leave their egg sac. It's called ballooning.

• It can be spun into a socklike tube. The purse web spider lives inside a silk tube. It has big fangs that allow it to bite prey right through the tube without going outside. Then it tears a hole in the tube to drag the prey inside.

• It can be used as a drag line. This is a thread the spider trails behind itself when it jumps from a high place. With this line, it can slow its fall. Also, it can climb back up the same line.

I recommend collecting spiders only when they're already dead, because many species help control pests. You can find dead spiders in corners and crevices outdoors when the weather turns cold; many species die off with the frost. Spiders that look dead may only be sluggish because of the cold. Before preserving a specimen, put it in a jar and let it stay indoors for a few hours. If it proves to be alive, let it go where you found it.

Depending on where you live, you may find a few species that are dangerous to people. I recommend leaving these alone. Check with the wildlife services or county extension agent in your area to find out which species to avoid. **Even some non-dangerous spiders can bite, so be careful.**

Spiders and harvestmen (see page 112) can't be preserved by pinning the way many insects can because their soft abdomens lose shape and fall off as they dry. That means they should be preserved with white vinegar. Put the spider in a vial, fill it all the way up with vinegar, and then shut the top tightly. Try not to open the vial again, because letting in air may encourage rot. The acid in the vinegar will keep germs from growing. With luck, the spider can last for years in vinegar. The vial will fit neatly in your cabinet.

Large spiders, such as tarantulas, can be preserved by freezing. Simply put the spider in a clear jar and stick it in the freezer. It will last about a year this way. With this method, you won't actually be able to keep the specimen in your cabinet most of the time. The good news is you can take it out of the freezer and handle it gently whenever you want. Just don't keep it out very long or it will thaw and smell bad. After a year or so, it will dry out. Its parts will break off easily. But the parts still won't rot. Dry things don't rot, and freezing for a long period dries things out.

You can also collect spider silk. You won't be able to keep the orb or other pattern intact, but the actual silk is collectible. Put a twig in the web and slowly roll it up. The silk will wrap around it. If there are dead insects in the web, they may cling to the twig with the silk. Put the whole twig into a clear plastic bag. You will find that different kinds of webs feel very different.

The most well-known use for a web is to catch insects and other prey. Even for this job, the silk can be used several different ways. Some spiders spin a fuzzy silk that catches prey by getting snagged on their own hairs, legs, or antennae. It is a bit like a Velcro fastener. Some spiders, called bolas spiders, put a good-smelling chemical in their silk. This chemical, called a pheromone, is the same one female moths use to attract males. The bolas spider makes a sticky ball of pheromone-laden silk and dangles it. When a male moth comes along, it touches the ball and gets stuck. Then the spider attacks. Still other spiders spin a tiny net they hold with their front legs. When an insect walks by, the spider throws the net on it and tangles it up.

ORB WEB SPIDERS

A common way of using silk to trap prey is the orb web. "Orb" means "circle." An orb web has strands of silk going out from the center in all directions, like the spokes on a bicycle wheel. Joining these spokes are spirals or circles of silk. Typically, orb-weavers repair their webs by eating the silk torn by insects or wind and spinning new strands to replace it. Some of these spiders eat and replace the entire web daily.

There are more than ten thousand kinds of orb web spiders. Many of them are fun to collect because they have bright colors.

Writing Spider *(Argiope aurantia)*

DOMAIN: EUKARYOTA
KINGDOM: ANIMALIA
PHYLUM: ARTHROPODA
CLASS: ARACHNIDA
ORDER: ARANEAE
FAMILY: ARANEIDAE
GENUS: *Argiope*
SPECIES: *A. aurantia*

The writing spider, also known as the yellow garden spider, builds a web the size of a car door. The female of the species can grow to more than an inch in body length. With the legs, it's much longer than that. Its cephalothorax is a silvery white. Its abdomen is black and yellow. Its legs are black striped with gold. (Males are smaller and less colorful.) They're called "writing spiders" because their orb webs are decorated with a big, fat zigzag of white silk called a stabilimentum. No one knows why they put this in their webs. It may help lure insects. It may be a sort of camouflage, making the spider's white body hard to spot against the white stabilimentum. Or it may help birds see the web, so they don't fly through it.

WHERE TO FIND Writing spiders are found in most tropical climates.

Golden Silk Orb Weaver
(Nephila clavipes)

DOMAIN: EUKARYOTA
KINGDOM: ANIMALIA
PHYLUM: ARTHROPODA
CLASS: ARACHNIDA
ORDER: ARANEAE
FAMILY: NEPHILIDAE
GENUS: *Nephila*
SPECIES: *N. clavipes*

This is one ugly spider. Its speckled, pale abdomen juts forward over its cephalothorax. It looks as if it has a humped back. Its yellow legs have bands of dark fur. As its name suggests, its silk is golden, not white. It's the strongest kind of spider silk—six times stronger than steel. Most spiders have a venom that kills insects, but does not hurt people. The golden silk orb weaver is an exception. Its bite can cause a swollen sore. However, it will only bite if a person grabs it.

WHERE TO FIND Golden silk orb weavers live in warm regions all over the world.

Cat-Faced Spider *(Araneus gemmoides)*

DOMAIN: EUKARYOTA
KINGDOM: ANIMALIA
PHYLUM: ARTHROPODA
CLASS: ARACHNIDA
ORDER: ARANEAE
FAMILY: ARANEIDAE
GENUS: *Araneus*
SPECIES: *A. gemmoides*

These orb weavers come in different color schemes, usually dominated by orange or brown. They like to make their webs near porch lights. The back end of this spider gives it its name. Two bumps protrude from its abdomen, like the ears of a cat. Behind these are some little dents that look like eyes. You wouldn't really mistake it for a cat. But some predators don't know what to make of it. They leave it alone.

WHERE TO FIND Cat-faced spiders are found in the US and Canada.

COBWEB SPIDERS

Orb webs are mostly flat. Cobwebs, or tangle webs, are different. They go in every direction. They don't have a pattern, like the orb does. To a human, they look like a mess. Most cobweb spiders don't take their webs down every day. Instead, they just fix any holes in the web. If a cobweb spider stays in one place for a long time, its web can grow as big as a coffee table. Underneath it, you may find lots of dead bugs. The spider has already sucked the juice out of them, then cut them loose from the web.

One common weaver of cobwebs is the American house spider (*Parasteatoda tepidariorum*). Its web often turns up in unused corners of homes, where it does a lot of good by eating pest insects. The female spider has a plump abdomen with brown and white markings. The male looks the same, except that its abdomen is much more slender. An adult male stores sperm in knobs at the tips of its pedipalps, or feelers. In fact, knobby palps distinguish the males in many spider species.

Tarantula (family Theraphosidae)

DOMAIN: EUKARYOTA
KINGDOM: ANIMALIA
PHYLUM: ARTHROPODA
CLASS: ARACHNIDA
ORDER: ARANEAE
FAMILY: THERAPHOSIDAE

Tarantulas make great exhibits for a cabinet. Because of their size, you can easily see features that are hard to spot on small spiders, like the spinnerets and the eyes. Tarantulas are big and hairy. They live in silk burrows (either in the ground or nestled in trees). The largest species, the goliath birdeater, has a leg span of up to 12 inches, which is big enough to span a soccer ball. Each species is different, but most use a venom that doesn't seriously harm people. Their bites are still painful because their fangs are large enough to stab like needles.

Tarantulas prey on insects and other small animals. They don't use a web as a snare; instead, they ambush prey. For example, the tarantula may wait inside its burrow until it feels the footsteps of a beetle vibrating the ground. The tarantula springs out of its burrow and seizes the beetle, biting it to inject venom. Besides the venom, the sheer force of the bite is often enough to kill an insect. The tarantula holds on to the prey for a long time, occasionally chewing it to work in more venom and digestive fluids. Like the housefly, the tarantula partly digests its food before swallowing it. The process of chewing digestive fluids in and sucking digested material down may take hours. In the end, the tarantula will leave a bundle of hard parts that it couldn't digest, held together with silk. In addition to insects, tarantulas have been known to eat earthworms, frogs, and, on rare occasions, small birds.

Tarantulas come in many colors. Wild species found in the US are usually dark brown, except for the tan cephalothorax.

WHERE TO FIND Tarantulas live all over the southern hemisphere and parts of the Nothern Hemisphere.

The Brazilian black tarantula

The Mexican redknee, which is sometimes kept as a pet, has a dark body with red, orange, or yellow stripes on its legs.

HARVESTMAN

DOMAIN: EUKARYOTA
KINGDOM: ANIMALIA
PHYLUM: ARTHROPODA
CLASS: ARACHNIDA
ORDER: OPILIONES

The harvestman, sometimes called a daddy longlegs, looks like a spider, but it's not. It's a relative of the spider. You can tell the difference because the harvestman has only one body section, not two. Its legs are long and stringy.

Harvestmen often hang out in groups. Sometimes thousands of them are found in a huge ball. If you poke the ball, the harvestmen will scatter in every direction. They will also make a horrible smell, like rotten bananas. The smell is supposed to make you go away.

The harvestman has another trick. When a predator grabs it, it sheds a leg on purpose. While the predator is grabbing the leg, the harvestman makes its getaway. The harvestman carries on just fine without its leg. It will use this trick on you, too, if you try to grab it.

WHERE TO FIND Dead or dying harvestmen are often found near water sources, such as outdoor faucets. They have to be handled carefully because the legs come off so easily. You can preserve them in vinegar, just like spiders.

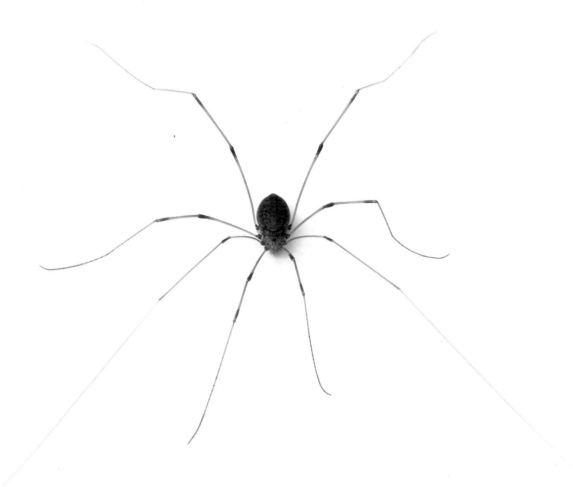

SCORPIONS

DOMAIN: EUKARYOTA
KINGDOM: ANIMALIA
PHYLUM: ARTHROPODA
CLASS: ARACHNIDA
ORDER: SCORPIONES

Like spiders, scorpions have eight legs. They also have pedipalps. On spiders, the pedipalps serve as feelers, much like the antennae of insects. In scorpions, they take the form of pincers, similar to those on a crab. A scorpion uses its pincers to seize its prey—mostly insects and spiders.

A scorpion also has a telson, or stinger, at the tip of its tail. The telson consists of a muscular bulb to produce and hold the venom and a needlelike barb for injecting it into prey. It may also use the stinger for defense against its enemies. In general, the bigger a scorpion is, the less it uses its sting on prey. Instead, it simply tears prey apart with its pincers and its powerful mouthparts. Big scorpions tend to have fairly mild venom because they don't need a strong one. For that reason, the bigger and scarier-looking a scorpion is, the less likely it is to harm people. (The biggest ones can reach eight inches in length.) Smaller scorpions with weak, slender pincers mostly rely on their venom to kill prey. They are likely to have a potent venom that can harm a human. A few of the 1,750 species can even kill a person.

Hundreds of years ago, people held an odd theory about the origin of scorpions. They thought venomous snakes didn't just decay when they died, but disintegrated into hundreds of scorpions! The truth is, scorpions come from eggs, like other arachnids. What's unusual about scorpions is that the mother keeps the eggs inside her body until they hatch. Then the young—scorplings, as they are called—emerge from her abdomen and ride on her body until they are old enough to take care of themselves.

WHERE TO FIND Scorpions can be found on every continent except Antarctica.

HOW TO COLLECT Since many scorpions have a dangerous sting, it's best not to collect them from the wild. But some people like to buy safer species, such as emperor scorpions, from a pet store. These big specimens can sting, but their venom is only about as dangerous as a bee's. They make good pets, and they can be preserved after they die by freezing them the same way you would a tarantula. (You might want to tell your family that not everything in the freezer is for eating.)

MEROSTOMATA

HORSESHOE CRABS

DOMAIN: EUKARYOTA
KINGDOM: ANIMALIA
PHYLUM: ARTHROPODA
CLASS: MEROSTOMATA
ORDER: XIPHOSURA
FAMILY: LIMULIDAE

Horseshoe crabs aren't really crabs, and they definitely aren't horseshoes. They get their name from what they look like. The legs and shells reminded people of both crabs and horseshoes. They are actually related to scorpions and spiders, although they are in a separate class.

A horseshoe crab has a round shell, nine eyes, ten legs, and a long tail. It almost never comes out on dry land, except to mate. It can live in a tide pool, which is a puddle at the edge of the ocean, or in a shallow part of the ocean itself. At high tide, the pool mixes with sea water. At low tide, the ocean ebbs, but some of its water stays in the pool. Tide pools are home to many interesting living things—hermit crabs, limpets, sea urchins, even some kinds of octopus. But the horseshoe crab is unique.

A horseshoe crab is soft but firm to the touch, like wet fingernails. Small ones are about the size of a quarter. The biggest ones are about 2 feet long. If you pick up a small one, it will kick its tiny legs to get away, tickling your palm.

The horseshoe crab is one of the oldest types of animals on earth. Scientists have discovered them in fossils that are 450 million years old. (People have only been here about three million years.) Never kill a horseshoe crab. In some places, like South Carolina, it is illegal to kill or collect them. But it's usually okay to collect empty exoskeletons you find on the beach. Like insects and spiders, the horseshoe crab sheds its old exoskeleton as it grows bigger.

WHERE TO FIND This ancient arthropod can be found on beaches and in shallow ocean waters throughout Southeast and East Asia. The American horseshoe crab can be found along the eastern coast of the US and in the Gulf of Mexico.

HORSESHOE CRABS HAVE BEEN WASHING UP
ON EARTH'S SHORES FOR 450 MILLION YEARS.

HOW TO CLEAN AND PRESERVE A HORSESHOE CRAB

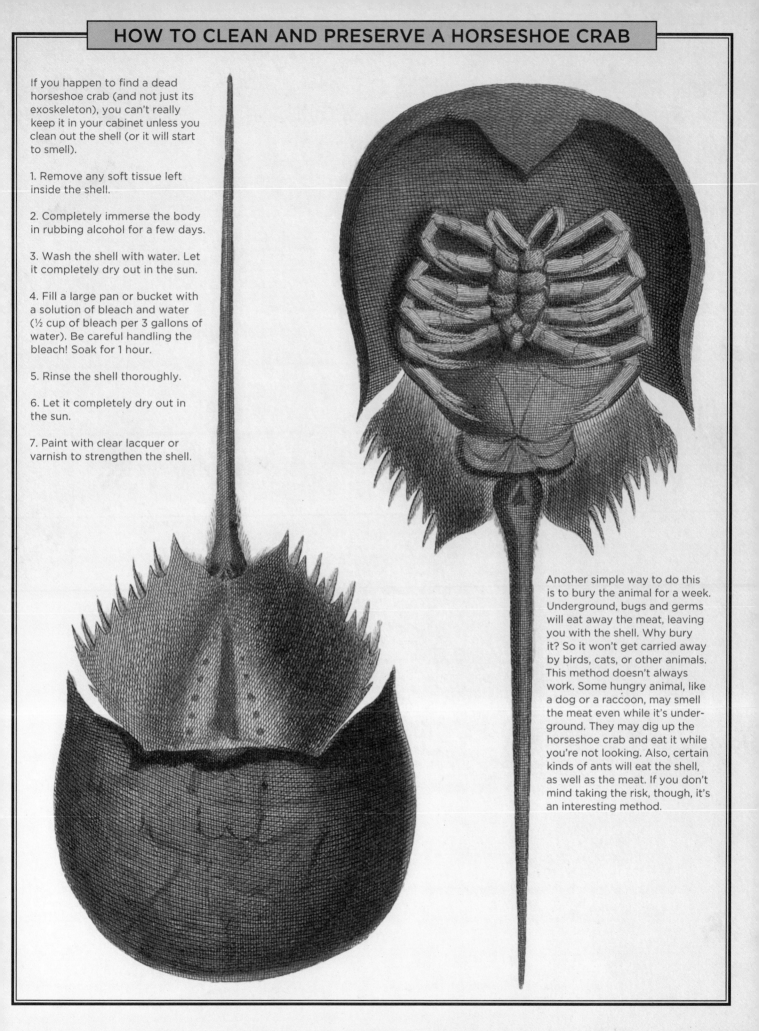

If you happen to find a dead horseshoe crab (and not just its exoskeleton), you can't really keep it in your cabinet unless you clean out the shell (or it will start to smell).

1. Remove any soft tissue left inside the shell.

2. Completely immerse the body in rubbing alcohol for a few days.

3. Wash the shell with water. Let it completely dry out in the sun.

4. Fill a large pan or bucket with a solution of bleach and water (½ cup of bleach per 3 gallons of water). Be careful handling the bleach! Soak for 1 hour.

5. Rinse the shell thoroughly.

6. Let it completely dry out in the sun.

7. Paint with clear lacquer or varnish to strengthen the shell.

Another simple way to do this is to bury the animal for a week. Underground, bugs and germs will eat away the meat, leaving you with the shell. Why bury it? So it won't get carried away by birds, cats, or other animals. This method doesn't always work. Some hungry animal, like a dog or a raccoon, may smell the meat even while it's underground. They may dig up the horseshoe crab and eat it while you're not looking. Also, certain kinds of ants will eat the shell, as well as the meat. If you don't mind taking the risk, though, it's an interesting method.

CRUSTACEA
(CRABS, LOBSTERS, SHRIMP, ETC.)

Crustaceans form a subphylum of arthropods that mostly live in the water. Like all arthropods, they have hard exoskeletons and jointed legs. Some of them differ from insects and spiders by having many appendages of different kinds—walking legs, swimming legs, feeding legs, several pairs of antennae, an array of mouthparts, tails with fans—and chelae, or claws.

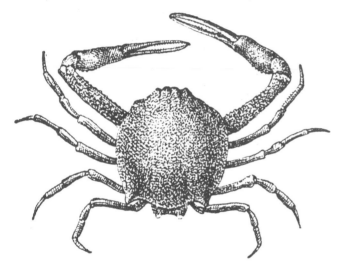

Most crustaceans are tiny. One shrimp-like species called ice krill is hardly more than an inch long. It lives in the coastal waters of the Antarctic, eating bacteria, algae, and other living or dead matter. It is sometimes found at depths of 13,000 feet. But ice krill are giants compared to the mostly microscopic crustaceans known as copepods. Copepods live in most of the waters of the world, but you have probably never seen one because they're rarely more than a couple of millimeters long. Under a microscope, a copepod looks like a teardrop with feathery antennae. It's so thin you can see right through it. On certain copepods that live at the bottom of bodies of water, scientists have found tiny parasites, less than one tenth of a millimeter long. It turns out these parasites, called *Stygotantulus stocki,* are also crustaceans. So far, they're the smallest known members of the group.

On the other hand, some crustaceans are huge. The largest, the Japanese spider crab, has a leg span of more than twelve feet. Besides crabs, other crustaceans that are often large enough to observe and collect include lobsters, shrimp, and crayfish. One group of crustaceans even lives on land—the wood lice, or sow bugs. These little animals are often found under rocks or rotting logs. You might mistake them for insects, but count the legs, and you'll find way too many—about fourteen. One family of wood louse, the pill bugs or roly polies, defend themselves by rolling into a ball.

CRABS

All the crustaceans we'll discuss in detail belong to the order Decapoda. That name reveals one defining characteristic of these crustaceans: "deca" means ten and "pod" means feet or legs. The ten legs of a decapod have specific jobs. The front three pairs are called maxillipeds. They are used as mouthparts, helpful for feeding and for handling objects. In many decapods, the front pair of maxillipeds has a chela, or claw. Those specialized maxillipeds are called chelipeds. The two hind pairs of legs are called pereiopeds. They are used for walking. Each leg has a gill for breathing.

What separates the crabs from other decapods? They usually have a single pair of chela, a short tail that's usually hidden beneath their body, and an extremely hard exoskeleton.

Fiddler Crab (genus *Uca*)

DOMAIN: EUKARYOTA
KINGDOM: ANIMALIA
PHYLUM: ARTHROPODA
SUBPHYLUM: CRUSTACEA
CLASS: MALACOSTRACA
ORDER: DECAPODA
FAMILY: OCYPODIDAE
GENUS: *Uca*

Fiddler crabs provide a clear case of sexual dimorphism. The females look symmetrical—the same on both sides. The males don't. One claw is much larger than the other. This oversized claw is a male's way of attracting females. (It also provides the animal's common name: Some people think it looks like a fiddle.) The male waves the claw in hopes that females will be impressed by it. The females generally choose the males with the biggest claws and those who wave their claws most energetically. The male also battles other males with it—this, too, is part of impressing the females.

Fiddlers live in burrows near salty bodies of water, such as the ocean or a brackish swamp. They're small—of the one hundred or so species, none grows bigger than 2 inches across. Fiddlers eat whatever they find lying around on the soil or sand—decomposing plants, dead animals, fungi, microbes, algae.

WHERE TO FIND Fiddler crabs are found in the temperate or warm oceans bordering the east and west coasts of North America, the Atlantic-facing countries of South America, Indo-West Pacific countries and islands, and parts of Africa and Asia.

Spiny Spider Crab

(Maja squinado)

DOMAIN: EUKARYOTA
KINGDOM: ANIMALIA
PHYLUM: ARTHROPODA
SUBPHYLUM: CRUSTACEA
CLASS: MALACOSTRACA
ORDER: DECAPODA
FAMILY: MAJIDAE
GENUS: *Maja*
SPECIES: *M. squinado*

The spiny spider crab's carapace is covered with rough spines. Two of the spines stick out between the eyes like horns. The crab is usually brown, orange, or red, but its shell may be covered with algae that disguises its true color. This is one of many species included among the spider crabs. They are called this because their proportions, with the legs especially long in comparison to the body, make them look like spiders. The spiny sea crab feeds on sea cucumbers, sea urchins, and other echinoderms, as well as mollusks and seaweed. When it needs to molt, it may travel hundreds of miles along the ocean bottom to congregate with others of its species. The spiny spider crabs pile themselves into mounds. In one case, fifty thousand of them were counted at the same site. The reason for these gatherings seems to be protection. The crabs are vulnerable to predators when they molt, but numbers make them safer—the predators can't attack them all.

WHERE TO FIND The spiny spider crab can be found in the waters off Europe, the northeast Atlantic Ocean, and in the Mediterranean Sea.

Japanese Blue Crab

(Portunus trituberculatus)

DOMAIN: EUKARYOTA
KINGDOM: ANIMALIA
PHYLUM: ARTHROPODA
SUBPHYLUM: CRUSTACEA
CLASS: MALACOSTRACA
ORDER: DECAPODA
FAMILY: PORTUNIDAE
GENUS: *Portunus*
SPECIES: *P. trituberculatus*

People often eat the delicious Japanese blue crab. Its most striking feature is its bright blue legs. Its carapace (the upper part of its shell) is usually brown or dull green with irregular blotches of lighter color. It's rough to the touch; it may even feel like sand. Many spikes protrude from its shell, including two long ones at its widest part. More spikes stick out like teeth along the front of the shell. Scientists count the "teeth" to tell the Japanese blue crab apart from similar species. There are even spikes on its chelipeds and claws.

WHERE TO FIND The Japanese blue crab can be found in the waters off the coasts of East Asia. It is the most popular species of crab to be fished.

•**118**•

Northern Kelp Crab
(Pugettia producta)

DOMAIN: EUKARYOTA
KINGDOM: ANIMALIA
PHYLUM: ARTHROPODA
SUBPHYLUM: CRUSTACEA
CLASS: MALACOSTRACA
ORDER: DECAPODA
FAMILY: EPIALTIDAE
GENUS: *Pugettia*
SPECIES: *P. producta*

These crabs are named for what they eat. Kelp are a group of seaweed known for their fast growth. The largest kinds can grow more than 19 inches per day. They can reach 260 feet long, forming undersea forests. The kelp look like plants, but they actually are brown algae, which don't belong in the plant kingdom. (Scientists are currently debating how to classify them.) The crabs feed on this abundant food. If they can't find kelp, they resort to small animals, like the little crustaceans called barnacles. A kelp crab is about 4 inches across at most. Its body is shaped like a policeman's badge. It's smooth except for a few spines shaped like the thorns of a rose—one at each side, another pair on the front corners of its carapace. Like all crabs, this one has a bit of carapace that extends forward between the eyes, called a rostrum. In kelp crabs, the rostrum forms two sharp points.

WHERE TO FIND The northern kelp crab can be found all along the western coast of North America—from southern Alaska to northern Mexico.

Brown Crab
(Cancer pagurus)

DOMAIN: EUKARYOTA
KINGDOM: ANIMALIA
PHYLUM: ARTHROPODA
SUBPHYLUM: CRUSTACEA
CLASS: MALACOSTRACA
ORDER: DECAPODA
FAMILY: CANCRIDEA
GENUS: *Cancer*
SPECIES: *C. pagurus*

This crab's shell is fluted at the edges like a pie. Coincidentally, it's also good for eating—in fact, another common name for it is "edible crab." As a youngster, its shell is brownish purple; as it matures, it turns reddish brown. The tips of its claws are black. Its maximum size is around 10 inches across, though most adults are considerably smaller than that. Brown crabs can live for one hundred years. The females can produce up to three million eggs at a time. The brown crab lives in a zone from the shallows of the ocean out to depths of 330 feet or so. To avoid predators, it often hides in the crevices of rocks or buries itself in the sand. It eats snails, bivalves, lobsters, and even smaller species of crabs. Humans aren't the only animals that eat brown crabs. Its main predators are octopuses.

WHERE TO FIND The brown crab is the most commonly fished crab in Western Europe, and it can be found in the North Sea and the northern Atlantic Ocean.

LOBSTERS

Several different decapods are called lobsters. Best known are the true lobsters (family Nephropidae) and the rock lobsters, also called spiny lobsters (family Palinuridae). Both have long, narrow bodies with muscular tails and, of course, ten legs. Both groups contain many edible species. They aren't closely related, but it will be handy to sort them out here.

What's the difference? True lobsters have claws on the first three pairs of legs. At a glance, most people only notice the front pair of claws, because they are much bigger. Often, this pair is so big you can crack the claws open to eat their meat, as well as that of the tail. Spiny lobsters usually have no noticeable claws. In many species, the female has a small claw on her hind leg; the males have none. The other big difference is the antennae. Both families have thin ones, but the spiny lobsters' antennae are far longer—generally longer than their own bodies.

Spiny Lobster
(family Palinuridae)

DOMAIN: EUKARYOTA
KINGDOM: ANIMALIA
PHYLUM: ARTHROPODA
SUBPHYLUM: CRUSTACEA
CLASS: MALACOSTRACA
ORDER: DECAPODA
FAMILY: PALINURIDAE

The long antennae of the spiny lobster are useful for tasting and touching. So powerful is the animal's sense of taste that it can actually navigate through the ocean by noticing the different taste of the salt water at different places. (It can also, through means not fully understood, sense the magnetic field of the earth and use it to navigate.) To scare away predators, the spiny lobster scrapes an antenna across a special rough spot on its shell. The result is a loud rasping noise. Yet another use of the antennae is to keep in touch with each other when dozens or hundreds of spiny lobsters go marching together across the floor of the ocean. It's like holding hands.

WHERE TO FIND Spiny lobsters can be found in shallow waters, tide pools, and coral reefs in the Caribbean Sea, the Mediterranean Sea, off the coast of South Africa, and in the warm waters of Australia and the South Pacific. They are not, taxonomically speaking, true lobsters.

WHEN LOBSTERS ARE ALIVE, THEY'RE USUALLY OLIVE GREEN OR BROWN, AND BLUE IN THEIR JOINTS. WHEN A LOBSTER IS BOILED, THE HEAT FROM THE WATER DISSOLVES A CERTAIN PIGMENT IN THE SHELL, AND THE LOBSTER TURNS BRIGHT RED AS A RESULT.

American Lobster (*Homarus americanus*)

DOMAIN: EUKARYOTA
KINGDOM: ANIMAL
PHYLUM: ARTHROPODA
SUBPHYLUM: CRUSTACEA
CLASS: MALACOSTRACA
ORDER: DECAPODA
FAMILY: NEPHROPIDAE
GENUS: *Homarus*
SPECIES: *H. americanus*

This is the largest of the clawed or "true" lobsters. I mentioned on page 116 that the Japanese spider crab is the world's largest crustacean—if you measure by its leg span. The American lobster doesn't cover nearly so much space, but, weighing a maximum of 44 pounds or so, it's the heaviest crustacean.

The lobster has olfactory sensors—organs for detecting smells—on its antennae and on the shorter feelers called antennules. By monitoring the water with these organs, it can detect objects in the ocean and tell their direction precisely. Lobsters use the sense of smell to communicate with each other as well. When a lobster detects another lobster approaching, it squirts urine into the water with great force. The stream of urine can project up to 7 feet. The second lobster can tell by smelling the urine whether the first one is male or female and whether it's interested in mating. This system is especially efficient because the lobster has two urinary bladders, one located on each side of its head.

An American lobster's claws don't match. The smaller one, called the cutter, is mostly for holding on to prey and tearing it into pieces. The larger claw, called the crusher, is for breaking through the hard shells of prey. The lobster eats mussels and other mollusks, sea urchins and other echinoderms, and bristle worms. It will eat many other things if it gets the chance, which is why fishermen can catch it by baiting their pots with herring.

Lobsters have come to be regarded as a delicacy, but that wasn't always the case. Up until the mid-1800s, only poor people and prisoners ate them. If you eat a lobster in a restaurant, your server will probably provide some special tools—a nutcracker-like pair of pliers and a slender fork. The pliers make it easier to get at the meat (which is mostly in the claws and tail), but you might chose to simply pick the meat out with a fork. This way, the shell remains intact for your cabinet.

WHERE TO FIND American lobsters can be found all along the Atlantic coast. They favor shallow waters with rocks and crevices to shield them from predators.

CRAYFISH, PRAWNS, AND SHRIMP

Crayfish—also called crawfish or crawdads—are related to lobsters. Not only are they both in the order Decapoda, but they're both in an infraorder called Asticidea. It's not surprising that they're related, because crayfish look like little lobsters. They're found in freshwater environments, such as rivers, ponds, or even mud puddles.

Classifying shrimp is a tricky matter. "Shrimp" is a common name that has no exact scientific equivalent. That's because people use "shrimp" to mean a number of different decapods, mostly in the families Dendrobrachiata and Caridea. Even though these animals aren't all closely related, they share some traits. Their general shape is like that of a lobster, with a long tail and noticeable antennae. Unlike lobsters, though, they do more swimming than walking, and their shape shows it. Their tails often curl under their bodies. Their legs are small and built for waving like fins in the water. These specialized swimming legs are called pleopods. Many shrimp can't walk at all, though they can use their legs to clutch a rock when at rest.

"Prawn" is another word for shrimp. In some places, it has a more specific meaning—for example, it may mean only the larger kinds of edible shrimp. But neither of these terms has a rigorously defined scientific meaning.

Crayfish (order Decapoda)

DOMAIN: EUKARYOTA
KINGDOM: ANIMALIA
PHYLUM: ARTHROPODA
SUBPHYLUM: CRUSTACEA
CLASS: MALACOSTRACA
ORDER: DECAPODA

Crayfish often live in burrows on the banks of streams. You can recognize a burrow by the tower of mud or stones around its opening. If a crayfish goes into its burrow, there's no point trying to dig it out. The burrow may be three feet deep, and its deeper end is under water. Other species of crayfish live under stones in the water. They dart out to feed, perhaps snatching a passing fish. When threatened, a crayfish propels itself backward to escape. It does this by flapping its tail. The escape happens surprisingly fast, much faster than the crayfish's normal forward swimming movements. Other crustaceans, including lobsters, shrimp, and krill, use this same escape trick.

WHERE TO FIND Crayfish are found in brooks, streams, swamps, and other sources of fresh water around the world.

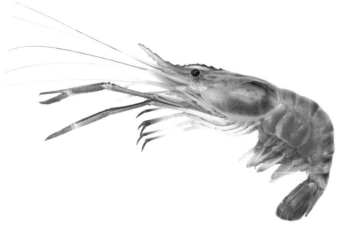

Giant River Prawn
(*Macrobrachium rosenbergii*)

DOMAIN: EUKARYOTA
KINGDOM: ANIMALIA
PHYLUM: ARTHROPODA
SUBPHYLUM: CRUSTACEA
CLASS: MALACOSTRACA
ORDER: DECAPODA
FAMILY: PALAEMONIDAE
GENUS: *Macrobrachium*
SPECIES: *M. rosenbergii*

All crustaceans go through a metamorphosis, much like insects do. What's unusual about giant river prawns is that, even after they have reached the adult stage, the males continue to change form. First, they are in the "small male" form. Their claws are tiny and clear. Later, they may develop into "orange claw" males, like the one shown in the picture above. Their claws not only change color, they also get bigger and the chelipeds (pincers) they are attached to get longer. If they develop further, they become "blue claw" males. Their claws have changed color and grown again, and their chelipeds get so long they begin to resemble Japanese spider crabs. Blue claw males are dominant. Each of them rules a territory and gets to mate with the females in it. The other males have fewer mating opportunities. They never develop into the bigger forms until the blue claw male in their territory dies.

WHERE TO FIND Giant river prawns are native to the Australian and Southeast Asian coasts.

Tiger Shrimp
(*Penaeus monodon*)

DOMAIN: EUKARYOTA
KINGDOM: ANIMALIA
PHYLUM: ARTHROPODA
SUBPHYLUM: CRUSTACEA
CLASS: MALACOSTRACA
ORDER: DECAPODA
FAMILY: ATYIDAE
GENUS: *Penaeus*
SPECIES: *P. monodon*

The tiger shrimp has stripes, as you might expect—black stripes. It's also called the bee shrimp because its pattern resembles that of a honeybee. This is what it usually looks like in the wild, and also in many aquariums. What makes it especially interesting for collectors is that it's been bred in captivity to have many color variants. For example, one variant sports orange eyes on a blue body. Another, called the crystal red shrimp, has broad red and white stripes. In their variety, they're like dogs. Think of the many shapes and colors of dogs, from the tiny, fragile Chihuahua to the burly 200-pound Saint Bernard to the slender greyhound built for speed. All of these dogs belong to the same species. People have bred them selectively to produce different shapes and sizes for different jobs. In the case of the shrimp, people have bred them for their beautiful colors. My favorite is the shadow panda. Its broad stripes alternate black and light blue.

WHERE TO FIND Tiger shrimp are native to Australia, Southeast Asia, the eastern African coast, and the Arabian Peninsula. They can also be found in the Gulf of Mexico.

HOW TO PRESERVE EXOSKELETONS, TAILS, AND PINCERS

The exoskeleton is the collectible part of a crustacean. To clean the shell, you can use the burial method I suggested for horseshoe crabs (on page 115).

Another method that works with a crab is to cook it, open the shell, and take out the meat. You will have to carefully break open the claws to get the meat out of them as well. After you cook it and scrape the meat out, you can dry it by packing the shell in salt. Fill the inside of the shell and claws with ordinary table salt or borax. Put them in a bowl and bury them in more salt. The crab should be totally covered. Leave it that way for a week. After that, it should be dried out. Brush the salt off and it's ready for your cabinet.

Some parts of your crustacean may not dry out well—for example, small legs. If they're soft enough to give when you pinch them yet too small to scrape the meat out of, you may have to throw them away. They can start to smell bad even after a salt treatment.

CHAPTER FOUR

PHYLUM
MOLLUSCA

Mollusks are mostly aquatic animals with soft, fleshy bodies. Many of them have shells. Familiar examples include octopuses, squids, snails, slugs, clams, mussels, and oysters. The body of a mollusk usually has three main sections. First, there's the head. It may not always be in the obvious place. For example, the head of an octopus is near the middle of its body. Second, there's the visceral mass.

"Viscera" are soft internal organs, like the stomach and intestines. In the case of mollusks, these tend to be packaged snugly together, often near the center of the body. Third, there's the foot, a muscular part used for moving around.

What really set most mollusks apart are the mantle and the radula. The radula is a mollusk's tongue. It tends to serve as a rasp, or file, for scraping food off a surface. For example, a snail can lick the algae from a stone with its radula. The giant land snail, which can grow to a diameter of more than

12 inches, can even lick the stucco from the walls of a house. The radula is made largely of chitin, the tough substance that also makes up most of the exoskeletons of arthropods. In some mollusks, the chitin is laced with magnetite, a mineral containing iron. That makes it an especially powerful rasp.

The mantle is the part of the mollusk's body wall (the outer layer of its body) on its dorsal, or back. It protects the visceral mass. It also contains a cavity. Inside this cavity, depending on the type of mollusk, you might find many different adaptations. Some mollusks, for example, have a siphon, or tube, inside the mantle cavity. It can suck water in for filter feeding (straining food particles from the water) or squirt water out for jet propulsion. On the outside, the mantle usually extends beyond the visceral mass, hanging like a loose garment. This outside part of the mantle can have the shape of wings or fins—as in the case of squid (it helps them swim). In clams and their relatives, the mantle secretes a substance that hardens into a shell.

Lettered Cone
Conus litteratus

Banded Tree Snail

Great Scallop
Pecten maximus

Dickey's Ear Abalone
Haliotis cuminata

Brown Turritella
Turritella terebra

Money Cowrie
Cypraea moneta

Sea Horse

Lion's Paw Clam
Pecten subnodosus

Brown Turritella
Turritella terebra

Arabian Cowrie
Cypraea arabica

Coral

Tesselate Cone
Conus tessulatus

Fox Shell
Fasciolaria trapezium

Star Fish

Gray Bonnet
Semicassis granulata

Marble Cone
Conus marmoreus

Radiate Top
Trochus radiatus

Endive murex
Murex endivia

Pecan Pecten
Gyroscala pyrum

Tiger Cowrie
Cypraea tigris

Noble Pecten
Pecten nobilis

Banded Tulip

Heart Cockle
Corculum cardissa

HOW TO PRESERVE YOUR MOLLUSK SHELLS

Seashells and other mementos from the ocean make for wonderful collecting. You can devote an entire cabinet to these treasures from the sea, and it's up to you how to organize them—whether by size or taxonomy or even color. As the following pages will show, although there's a tendency to arrange all marine shell life into one group, there are different classes and species to which these shells belong. One thing is true of all of them, however: A shell is the remnant of something that once lived inside of it. When you collect shells on the beach, remember to avoid taking any shells that are still occupied by living marine life. And remember, even empty shells may have been recently inhabited, so take the following precautions to ensure there is no animal tissue left inside that may make your seashell cabinet take on a "fishy" ocean smell.

1. Just to make sure your seashell is perfectly clean, boil it in a pot of water for about ten minutes. You can also pop it into the microwave if you don't mind the smell.

2. After your seashell has completely cooled from being either boiled or microwaved, let it soak in a 50-50 solution of bleach and water for a day or two. This will clear away any residual algae or periostracum, which is the flaky substance that covers most live seashells.

3. If after bleaching you want to clean it even further, try using a toothbrush—with toothpaste!—to scrub off any lingering dirt or grime. A toothpick is good, too, for cleaning out any nooks or crevices.

4. If there are any sharp points on your shell, it's okay to file them down with a nail file or sandpaper.

5. You can brush mineral oil over the seashell to add shine. Not too much: Just enough for a light coating that will give your seashell a beautiful natural-looking luster. Allow the shells to dry for at least one full day before handling.

6. This part is optional: You can spray the shells with satin-finish polyurethane, or coat with clear nail polish. This will make them more durable and add more luster.

These instructions work for most seashells in the phylum Mollusca. For sand dollars and other marine life, instructions vary.

GASTROPODA
(SNAILS AND SLUGS)

Gastropods comprise the snails and slugs. Members of this class are not symmetrical: The two sides of their bodies don't grow at the same rate, so as the body develops, it twists. By the time it's an adult, the gastropod's anus is above its head, pointing in the same direction. You can't readily see this odd development from the outside, though. What you usually see is a soft body, longer than it is wide, with two or four antennae projecting from its head. These antennae will retract when touched. They carry the organs the gastropod uses to smell. They may also carry eyes, either at the tip or at the base.

Gastropods with shells are called snails. The mantle of a snail is usually inside its shell, though you may see a bit of it sticking out. Gastropods without shells are called slugs. You may see the mantle of a slug on its back; it often has a noticeably different texture from the rest of the body. The terms *snail* and *slug* are merely descriptive. They don't reflect the relationships of the animals to each other. For example, one family might contain both snails and slugs.

There are tens of thousands of species of gastropoda. Most of them live in the ocean, and of the ones that don't, most live in lakes and other freshwater bodies. However, there are still many species who live on land and at shorelines. Snails that live on land are more likely to have a lung, rather than a gill, for breathing. Snails that live in the water are more likely to have an operculum—a lid for closing the shell when they hide inside it. People often use terms like "land snail" and "sea slug" to distinguish where the different species are found. These terms, too, are merely descriptive. Gastropods from sea and land can be closely related.

Since gastropods have soft bodies, they tend to decay rapidly after death. The only collectible part, really, is the shell. Snail shells typically grow in spiral shapes. Some are more like cones, and some look like flattened cones. All of these shapes come in a wide variety of colors, making them popular with collectors.

Garden Snail (*Cornu aspersum*)

DOMAIN: EUKARYOTA
KINGDOM: ANIMALIA
PHYLUM: MOLLUSCA
CLASS: GASTROPODA
ORDER: STYLOMMATOPHORA
FAMILY: HELICIDAE
GENUS: *Cornu*
SPECIES: *C. aspersum*

This common snail has a gray or brown body, sometimes speckled with white. Its shell comes in a variety of colors and patterns, with brown and yellow often dominating. A garden snail eats a variety of plants, including garden vegetables, fruit, and grains.

This snail has an interesting defense mechanism: It exudes slime. Ants that try to eat the snail can be overwhelmed and even drowned in this slime. Larger predators may simply find it distasteful. Since it's a land snail, it has no operculum. Instead, it uses a thin layer of slime to seal the door of its shell when it's at rest. The slime dries into a membrane called an epiphragm. Though larger animals can break through the membrane, it does keep some insects out.

The garden snail is a hermaphrodite. That means it's both male and female. When two of them mate, each fertilizes the eggs of the other. Each snail fires a tiny projectile called a love dart into the other's body. The dart is made of chitin and covered with a hormone that mingles with the recipient's blood. This hormone tells the recipient's body not to digest the sperm it will receive during mating, but to store it for fertilization.

WHERE TO FIND Garden snails are native to the Mediterranean region and Western Europe; however, they have been spread, primarily by humans, to much of the US, the western coast of Canada, Mexico, Chile, Argentina, Australia, and New Zealand.

Red Abalone (*Haliotis rufescens*)

DOMAIN: EUKARYOTA
KINGDOM: ANIMALIA
PHYLUM: MOLLUSCA
CLASS: GASTROPODA
ORDER: ARCHAEOGASTROPODA
FAMILY: HALIOTIDIDAE
GENUS: *Haliotis*
SPECIES: *H. rufescens*

Red abalones, a species of sea snail, live along the shore or in shallow water, where they cling to rocks. They eat kelp. Their main predators are people and otters. Diving for them is a popular sport. A red abalone shell can be more than a foot across. It's brick red or pink on the outside. Because it's shaped like a human ear, you can also see the inside, which is lined with a smooth material called nacre, or mother-of-pearl. Nacre is a gleaming white. Other colors, like pink, green, and gold, seem to shine through the white. You may have to tilt the shell at different angles to see these other colors. Three or four pores penetrate the shell; the abalone breathes through them. Abalones mate by releasing their sperm into the water. They don't even have to touch each other.

WHERE TO FIND Sea snails are found along the western coast of North America, from British Columbia to Baja California.

BIVALVIA
(CLAMS, OYSTERS, MUSSELS)

The bivalves include oysters, clams, mussels, scallops, and their relatives. Most of them have two shells to enclose their soft bodies—in fact, "bivalvia" means "two shells." (A few exceptions have evolved out of shells; these look like worms.) Bivalves typically feed by filtering food out of the water. To do this, they suck the water in through their gills. The gills are protected by mucus and hairlike organs called cilia. Particles in the water get trapped in the mucus. The cilia sort it out. Some particles are unusable junk, like grains of sand. The cilia push these out. Whatever's edible gets pushed into the mouth.

I said before that most mollusks have a head, but bivalves are exceptions to that. They don't have radulas, either. A bivalve does have a mantle, a visceral cavity, and a muscular foot. As you look at the animal, though (assuming you've opened its shell), your first impression will likely be a smear of slime. The only organs likely to stand out clearly are the gills. Since the bivalve uses them for both breathing and eating, they are typically large. You may recognize them by the cilia, which sometimes make them look feathery.

Of course, the most recognizable feature of a bivalve is the shell. The two parts are held together by a ligament that stiffens to open the shell. Powerful muscles, called adductors, pull the shell shut for protection. In the water, a bivalve often rests with its shell slightly open while it feeds. Some bivalves swim by flapping their shells like wings. Many species, however, don't move around much. They may burrow under the sediment beneath the water. They may anchor themselves with cords as fine as spider silk. Or they may glue themselves to a rock.

More than ten thousand bivalves are known to science, and many of them produce collectible shells. The shells of some bivalves are lined with nacre. Some of them, such as oysters, produce pearls. This happens when an irritant, such as a grain of sand, finds its way into the shell. The bivalve coats it with nacre to make it smooth and stop the irritation.

Quahog Clam (*Mercenaria mercenaria*)

DOMAIN: EUKARYOTA
KINGDOM: ANIMALIA
PHYLUM: MOLLUSCA
CLASS: BIVALVIA
ORDER: VENEROIDA
FAMILY: VENERIDAE
GENUS: *Mercenaria*
SPECIES: *M. mercenaria*

These clams reach a maximum of about 4 inches across. They burrow just below the sand at the shore. A quahog can travel to a new location by pushing with its muscular foot. On the outside, its shell is gray or white with dark arcs. Inside, it's sometimes purple. In older times, the Narragansett tribe and other Native peoples used the shells to make money. People often eat the quahog (for example, in clam chowder). It is the longest-living single animal known, with one specimen recorded at 507 years of age.

WHERE TO FIND Quahog clams are native to the eastern shores of North and Central America, from Prince Edward Island to the Yucatán Peninsula. They are common throughout New England, north into Canada, and all down the Eastern seaboard of the US to Florida.

Pacific Oyster (*Crassostrea gigas*)

DOMAIN: EUKARYOTA
KINGDOM: ANIMALIA
PHYLUM: MOLLUSCA
CLASS: BIVALVIA
ORDER: OSTREOIDA
FAMILY: OSTREIDAE
GENUS: *Crassostrea*
SPECIES: *C. gigas*

The Pacific oyster grows to about 8 inches across. Its shell is typically white, yellow, or grayish purple. It may be mottled with brighter bits of purple. Its shape is often crenellated, like the gathers in a curtain. Like many bivalves, it has a larval form that swims free, but as an adult, it stays put, gluing itself to a rock or other substrate in shallow water. It may even attach itself to the shell of other bivalves. The average Pacific oyster starts out as a male, but turns female later in life. It may switch back and forth several more times in its lifetime. It may even become both genders at once—a hermaphrodite.

WHERE TO FIND Pacific oysters are native to the Pacific Ocean around Eastern Asia, specifically Japan, Korea, and China, but have been introduced to Australia, New Zealand, the western coast of North America, and the Atlantic coast of Europe.

Freshwater Pearl Mussel
(*Margaritifera margaritifera*)

DOMAIN: EUKARYOTA
KINGDOM: ANIMALIA
PHYLUM: MOLLUSCA
CLASS: BIVALVIA
ORDER: UNIONOIDA
FAMILY: MARGARITIFERIDAE
GENUS: *Margaritifera*
SPECIES: *M. margaritifera*

This bivalve provides one of the great visual contrasts in the animal kingdom. On the outside, its shell is black or brownish, often crusted with literally hundreds of years of mineral deposits as well as live algae. It may look corroded. Inside, it's thickly coated with iridescent nacre. As its name implies, this species often makes beautiful pearls. It lives in fast-flowing rivers and streams. As a larva, it lives by filter-feeding inside a salmon or other type of fish. To get there, it swims free until the fish inhales it, then clamps its tiny shell shut on a bit of the fish's gill tissue. When it is big enough, it leaves the fish and lives partly buried in gravel or sand on the riverbed.

WHERE TO FIND Freshwater pearl mussels can be found in both the Arctic and temperate regions of western Russia, as well as throughout Europe, and in northeastern North America.

CEPHALOPODA
(CUTTLEFISH, OCTOPUSES, SQUID, NAUTILUSES)

Cephalopoda include squid, octopuses, cuttlefish, and nautiluses. These mollusks all have well-developed heads and large brains. They are considered the most intelligent invertebrates on earth. Some captive specimens have figured out how to open tricky locks in aquariums and have actually escaped! Others have figured out how to open jars and doors, or how to operate light switches. Many cephalopods have evolved beyond the need for external shells. Some have no shell at all, while others have a vestigial shell inside their bodies. Cuttlefish are distinguished from other cephalapods by their well-developed interior shell, called a cuttle. Octopuses are distinguished by having eight arms. Squid, like cuttlefish, have ten arms—including two longer arms called tentacles. Nautiluses can have up to ninety tentacles. Nautiluses are also the only cephalopods that have exterior shells. As such, they are the only cephalopoda that are able to be preserved in your collection.

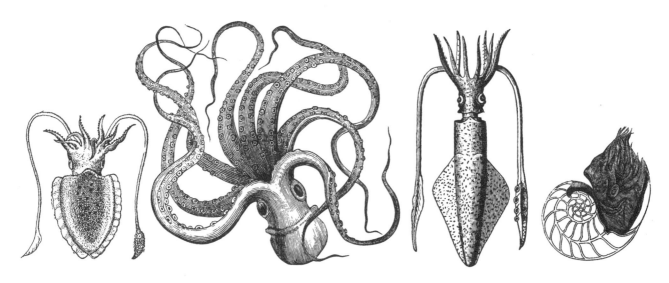

Cuttlefish have shells on the inside of their bodies.

Octopuses have no shells on the inside or outside of their bodies. They have eight legs.

Squid have ten legs—including the two long tentacles.

Nautiluses have exterior shells and up to ninety tentacles.

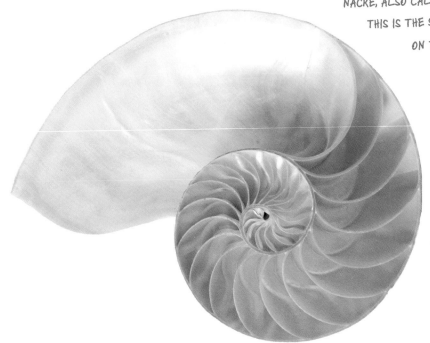

Nautilus *(Nautilus pompilius)*

DOMAIN: EUKARYOTA
KINGDOM: ANIMALIA
PHYLUM: MOLLUSCA
CLASS: CEPHALOPODA
ORDER: NAUTILIDA
FAMILY: NAUTILIDAE
GENUS: *Nautilus*
SPECIES: *N. pompilius*

When one of these mollusks feels threatened, it draws itself completely into its shell, just as some snails do. Then it covers the entrance to the shell with two specially flattened tentacles. Each of its many tentacles can itself be drawn into a fleshy sheath. When they're extended, they surround its mouth, like a beard or a mass of spaghetti it can't quite swallow. The mouth itself has a beak like a parrot's. Nautiluses generally eat carrion (dead animals), but they will also eat small marine animals when they come across them. The biggest nautiluses grow to more than 10 inches across.

The shell of a nautilus is dull outside, but lined with a glistening, iridescent nacre. The nautilus's shell is made up of a series of separate chambers. The nautilus always lives in a chamber just big enough to hold it when it retreats from danger. When it grows too big for a chamber, it walls up that one and builds a new, larger one. The wall that closed up the old chamber becomes the back of the new chamber. This new chamber has the same shape as the old one—a sort of curved box. Because of the curve, the chambers soon accumulate into a spiral. Each loop of the spiral is bigger than the one before it in a mathematically predictable way. The shape of the loop stays the same as they get bigger. This pattern is called a logorithmic spiral. It occurs in many natural phenomena—the shape of spiral galaxies, the way sand is deposited in certain bays, the flight path of a moth to light, even the approach of a hawk to a squirrel it's hunting!

WHERE TO FIND Generally found in the western Pacific Ocean, they often live near coral reefs or on the ocean floor at depths of up to 550 yards, but sometimes come to shallower waters at night.

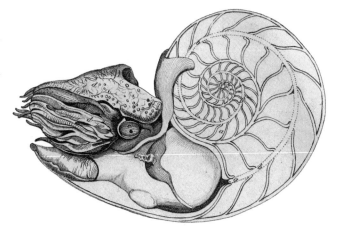

Nautiluses have less complex brains than other cephalopods—perhaps because they are the most closely related to the first cephalopods that appeared on earth 500 million years ago.

CHAPTER FIVE

PHYLA

ECHINODERMATA, CNIDARIA, AND PORIFERA

These three phyla really aren't in the same category. The animals in each phylum are vastly different from one another, and aren't any more closely related to each other than humans are to squids. What they do have in common, though, is that they are found easily along seashores, which makes them very collectible. Echinoderms include starfish, sand dollars, and sea urchins, which are easy to preserve. Cnidarians include jellyfish, and other noncollectible creatures, plus corals, which are not only amazing to look at, but also among the most durable objects you can have in your collection. Poriferans are sponges, which come in many colors and shapes.

ECHINODERMATA
(STARFISH, SEA STARS, SEA URCHINS)

Echinoderms are a group of marine animals including starfish, crinoids, brittle stars, sea urchins, sand dollars, and sea cucumbers. As adults, they have radial symmetry. This means that, instead of having a left and right side roughly identical to each other, they are built in sections like the slices of a pie, with each section identical to the others. Most echinoderms have five radial sections. This pattern is easy to see in many starfish, for example, because each of the five sections has its own arm.

Echinoderms typically have hard particles of calcite in their skins. This mineral gives the animal a sort of skeleton that remains after it dies. The skeleton is the collectible part. Another common trait of echinoderms is regeneration. If it loses an arm, the animal can grow it back. Some echinoderms can even grow the rest of the body back from the severed arm.

STARFISH (SEA STARS)

There are more than 1,500 species of starfish, which are also called sea stars. They come in a variety of colors, from bright orange to blue to pale pink to brown. Many of them have the typical echinoderm pattern, with five radially symmetrical sections, each sprouting one arm, or ray. Some species, though, have more than twenty arms.

Most starfish eat clams and other bivalves. To manage this, the starfish forces the clam's shell open with its strong arms. As soon as there's even a narrow opening—say, one millimeter wide—the starfish turns its stomach inside out and thrusts it through the crack. The stomach then uses acid to begin digesting the clam inside the shells. The clam soon weakens and the starfish is able to open the shell fully. It pulls its stomach back into itself and swallows the clam. Starfish may also eat various other small animals, such as snails, corals, worms, and sponges. Some species eat carrion and even feces.

The preserved skeleton of a starfish feels like rough rock. Most of them are durable and can be handled freely.

Common Starfish (*Asterias rubens*)

DOMAIN: EUKARYOTA
KINGDOM: ANIMALIA
PHYLUM: ECHINODERMATA
CLASS: ASTEROIDEA
ORDER: FORCIPULATIDA
FAMILY: ASTERIIDAE
GENUS: *Asterias*
SPECIES: *A. rubens*

This starfish has thick arms that taper toward the ends. Each arm is lined with a single row of spines. These animals can grow to 22 inches across, but more often they're less than 12. Their color is typically orange, brick red, or brown. The deeper they live in the water, the paler in color they are likely to be.

WHERE TO FIND Common starfish can be found throughout the Atlantic Ocean, the North Sea, and the Gulf of Mexico.

Horned Starfish (*Protoreaster nodosus*)

DOMAIN: EUKARYOTA
KINGDOM: ANIMALIA
PHYLUM: ECHINODERMATA
CLASS: ASTEROIDEA
ORDER: VALVATIDA
FAMILY: OREASTERIDAE
GENUS: *Protoreaster*
SPECIES: *P. nodosus*

This starfish has horns growing from its back, with the tallest horns near the center. These horns serve to intimidate predators. Sometimes they break off or erode. The animal sometimes has a tan body with darker horns, which has inspired some people to call it the chocolate chip sea star—because it looks like a cookie.

WHERE TO FIND Horned starfish are most common in warm, shallow waters, particularly in the Indo-Pacific region. They prefer soft, sandy, or muddy ocean floors, and are often spotted in or near sea grass.

Small Spine Sea Star (*Echinaster spinulosus*)

DOMAIN: EUKARYOTA
KINGDOM: ANIMALIA
PHYLUM: ECHINODERMATA
CLASS: ASTEROIDEA
ORDER: SPINULOSIDA
FAMILY: ECHINASTERIDAE
GENUS: *Echinaster*
SPECIES: *E. spinulosus*

This starfish has rows of spines running along its arms for protection. It is usually purple or brown. In a living specimen, you'll be able to spot other colorful features. The little tube feet under its arms with which it moves around and seizes prey have brilliant orange suckers at their tips. At the tips of its arms there are orange spots. These are light-sensitive organs—primitive eyes.

WHERE TO FIND The small spine sea star is found in shallow areas of the western Atlantic Ocean, the Caribbean Sea, and the Gulf of Mexico.

Spiny Starfish (*Marthasterias glacialis*)

DOMAIN: EUKARYOTA
KINGDOM: ANIMALIA
PHYLUM: ECHINODERMATA
CLASS: ASTEROIDEA
ORDER: FORCIPULATIDA
FAMILY: ASTERIIDAE
GENUS: *Marthasterias*
SPECIES: *M. glacialis*

These starfish have slender arms with orderly rows of spines. The central disk of a spiny starfish is small; it looks as if it's all arms. They can grow to more than two feet across. Though spiny starfish thrive in many different spots, from muddy shallows to wave-washed rock faces, they do best in calm waters; that's often where the biggest specimens are found.

WHERE TO FIND Spiny starfish are primarily found in deep waters off the western and southwestern coasts of the British Isles.

SEA URCHINS AND SAND DOLLARS

A typical live sea urchin looks like a ball with long spikes sticking out of it. The spikes are for protection. An animal that tries to bite or seize the urchin will get stabbed. Sometimes the spines break off in the attacker's flesh.

Some species of sea urchin have toxins in their spines. Occasionally, people get hurt by stepping on an urchin. The spines have to be removed entirely to avoid serious injury.

Some urchins also have organs called pedicellariae. These are like tentacles with mouths at the ends. In some species, the pedicellariae can also deliver toxins.

A sea urchin has an internal skeleton made of the mineral calcium carbonate. This skeleton is called a test. People sometimes refer to it as a shell, because urchin tests are often found on the beach with seashells. However, it's not a shell in the usual sense, because it lies beneath the animal's skin. It serves to protect the internal organs. It also anchors the spines. The test can last long after the animal dies; it's the collectible part of the animal. Sometimes, you can even see the five teeth of a sea urchin in its test—its mouth is on the bottom of its body in the center. Most tests clearly reveal the animal's five-fold radial symmetry, though it may not be obvious when the animal is alive. The sun often bleaches a test white, so that's the color you're most likely to find.

HOW TO PRESERVE SAND DOLLARS AND STARFISH

Sand dollars, starfish, and the other collectibles in this section are usually very fragile—and sometimes sharp. Handle with care. To preserve them, follow these instructions.

SAND DOLLARS

1. Soak in freshwater, changing the water every few hours, for a day or so. Continue to do this until the water stays fairly clear after soaking. Let dry thoroughly.

2. Soak for fifteen minutes in a solution of 50 percent bleach and 50 percent water. Do not soak them for too long, though, since the bleach contains chemicals that weaken the surface. Always be careful when handling bleach.

3. Remove from bleach solution and rinse thoroughly in water.

4. Let dry completely.

5. This part is optional: Paint them white or, to make them harden even more, apply a mixture of 50 percent glue and 50 percent water. Then let dry throroughly.

STARFISH

1. Soak in 70 percent isopropyl alcohol overnight. This should be enough to clean them completely.

2. Lay on plate, sprinkle a generous amount of natural sea salt on top, and allow to dry in the sun.

Common Sea Urchin SKELETON
(*Echinus esculentus*)

DOMAIN: EUKARYOTA
KINGDOM: ANIMALIA
PHYLUM: ECHINODERMATA
CLASS: ECHINOIDEA
ORDER: ECHINOIDA
FAMILY: ECHINIDAE
GENUS: *Echinus*
SPECIES: *E. esculentus*

In life, this species is usually red or purple with some white coloring among the spines. It has many short spines and a few long ones. Its test typically comprises twenty rows of stony plates. A common sea urchin is shaped like a globe flattened at the top and bottom. The female can produce 20 million eggs at one time, releasing them into the water. People use the common sea urchin as food.

WHERE TO FIND The common sea urchin is found mainly in the North Sea, as well as the western and northern coasts of Europe, from Portugal to Finland, Denmark, and Iceland.

Sea Biscuit
(*Clypeaster humilis*)

DOMAIN: EUKARYOTA
KINGDOM: ANIMALIA
PHYLUM: ECHINODERMATA
SUBPHYLUM: ELEUTHEROZOA
CLASS: ECHINOIDEA
SUBCLASS: EUECHINOIDEA
ORDER: CLYPEASTEROIDA
SUBORDER: CLYPEASTERINA
FAMILY: CLYPEASTERIDAE
GENUS: *Clypeaster*
SPECIES: *C. humilis*

The mouth of an urchin is underneath its body. And in most cases, its anus is on the opposite side—that is, right on top. The sea biscuits are exceptions—in their case, both mouth and anus are beneath its body. What's on top in this particular species of sea biscuit, as in several of its relatives, is a pattern like a flower with five petals. This pattern is made of specialized tube feet the animal uses for breathing. The flower pattern is visible even in the test.

WHERE TO FIND Though fossils of organisms in the *Clypeaster* genus can be found worldwide, *Clypeaster humilis* can be found in oceans around eastern and southern Africa, particularly around South Africa and Madagascar, and in the Red Sea.

Common Sand Dollar
(*Echinarachnius parma*)

DOMAIN: EUKARYOTA
KINGDOM: ANIMALIA
PHYLUM: ECHINODERMATA
CLASS: ECHINOIDEA
ORDER: CLYPEASTEROIDA
SUBORDER: SCUTELLINA
FAMILY: ECHINARACHNIIDAE
GENUS: *Echinarachnius*
SPECIES: *E. parma*

Sea biscuits are flat as cookies, but their cousins the sand dollars are even flatter than that. They're named for their resemblance to dollar coins. In life, they wear a coating of fine, velvety spines. They like parts of the ocean with soft sand or mud for burrowing. Sand dollar larvae have an unusual way of escaping predators. They quickly clone themselves. With two larvae trying to escape instead of one, their chances of at least one surviving are doubled.

WHERE TO FIND Common sand dollars are most often found on the eastern coast of North America north of New Jersey, but can also sometimes be found in the northern Pacific Ocean off the coast of Alaska and even Siberia and Japan.

PHYLUM

CNIDARIA
(JELLYFISH, CORAL, AND THEIR KIN)

CORAL BELONG TO THE CLASS ANTHOZOA.

Animals in the phylum Cnidaria come in a variety of shapes. At different stages of its metamorphosis, a cnidarian may appear to be either a wormlike polyp or a blob of jelly, and perhaps it will be ringed with tentacles.

The defining trait of the group is a tiny weapon called a nematocyst. This structure is like a gun that fires from a cell when it is stimulated by touch or by certain chemicals. A nematocyst can serve many purposes—capturing prey, defending against predators, attacking territorial rivals. It can come in several forms, too. Some are like harpoons, penetrating an enemy's body to deliver toxins. Others are tipped with a gluelike substance or a sort of lasso for holding on to the victim. In some form or other, nematocysts are found in all members of the phylum Cnidaria—jellyfish and box jellies, Portuguese men-of-war and other hydrozoans, fireweeds, sea anemones, corals, and fire corals. Some of these animals, particularly among the box jellyfish, can kill people with the toxins in their nematocysts.

What's safe to collect, though, are the homes made by a class of Cnidarians called corals. Each coral is a tiny polyp with tentacles fringing its mouth. In some species, millions of them live together as a colony, each making a tubelike shell of calcium carbonate to protect itself. They attach their shells to rocks or to each other. This communal home can grow into different colors and shapes.

Over a period of decades, the mass of connected shells made by some species of coral can form a huge underwater structure called a reef. The largest coral reef in the world is the Great Barrier Reef of Australia, formed by more than 3,000 coral colonies whose reefs eventually grew together. This super-reef is 1,260 miles long. Reefs like this are ecologically important; they provide shelter for many living things besides corals—fish, crustaceans, algae, and more. Along a reef, species-rich ecosystems form—ecosystems different from those in the surrounding water. It's estimated that one fourth of all marine species live on and around reefs, even though reefs account for far less than one percent of the oceans' area.

Branch Coral
(*Acropora florida*)

DOMAIN: EUKARYOTA
KINGDOM: ANIMALIA
PHYLUM: CNIDARIA
CLASS: ANTHOZOA
ORDER: SCLERACTINIA
FAMILY: ACROPORIDAE
GENUS: *Acropora*
SPECIES: *A. florida*

This coral belongs to a group that are called the staghorns, because of their branching, hornlike pattern. They grow rapidly, allowing them to form reefs as they crowd out slower-growing kinds of coral. Because branch coral is light and fragile, it breaks easily in storms.

Branch corals share their shells with a type of algae called zooxanthellae. The coral feeds on the food the algae produce by photosynthesis. (It also uses its nematocysts to sting and eat various tiny floating animals—zooplankton— from the water.) In return, the algae get shelter and the use of the coral's nutritious waste products. This kind of mutually beneficial relationship between two species is called symbiosis.

WHERE TO FIND Branch coral is found in the Indo-Pacific region, ranging from the waters around Japan and eastern China to coral reefs near Australia to the southwest Indian Ocean.

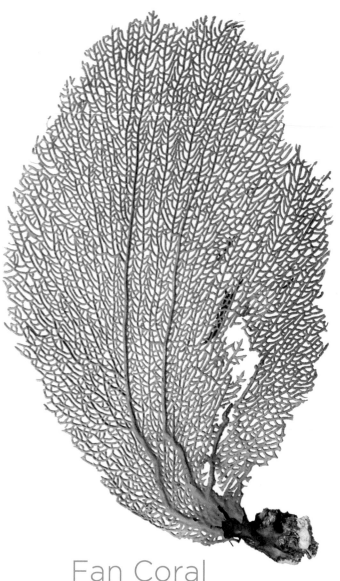

Brain Coral
(family Faviidae)

DOMAIN: EUKARYOTA
KINGDOM: ANIMALIA
PHYLUM: CNIDARIA
CLASS: ANTHOZOA
ORDER: SCLERACTINIA
SUBORDER: FAVIINA
FAMILY: FAVIIDAE

The shells of these corals typically grow into a sturdy, rounded shape like a cauliflower or, as the name suggests, a human brain. This shape takes much longer to grow than branch coral, but it is hard to crack. As a result, brain coral structures can live in fast currents. They can even withstand hurricanes. The shapes and colors of species in the family vary quite a bit, though, as evidenced by such common names as pineapple coral, moon coral, and candy cane coral. They may grow to six feet high and live nine hundred years. They grow atop and beside each other to form reefs.

Brain corals live in symbiosis with zooxanthellae, but they also prey on zooplankton. They are large for corals, so they can even sting and prey on animals as big as brine shrimp. But their nematocysts aren't just for catching prey: They use them to kill other species of coral in order to protect their living space.

WHERE TO FIND Brain coral can be found in any area that contains shallow, warm-water coral reefs, which are present in all the world's oceans.

Fan Coral
(order Alcyonacea)

DOMAIN: EUKARYOTA
KINGDOM: ANIMALIA
PHYLUM: CNIDARIA
CLASS: ANTHOZOA
ORDER: ALCYONACEA

These animals, also known as gorgonians, have eight tentacles around their mouths. The tentacles wave plankton in from the water. The colony, and thus the collectible shell, takes on the shape of a leaf or fan. It's broad, but not deep, and usually anchored like a plant in sediment or to a stone. This shape, with its large surface area, is ideal for a colony that needs to filter its food from the water. The gorgonian may provide a home for other animals, such as sea horses and brittle stars.

The fans come in an array of colors, from deep purple to bright red.

WHERE TO FIND There are over five hundred species of Alcyonacea, but they are mainly found in warm, shallow waters around the Caribbean, particularly Florida, Bermuda, and the West Indies.

PORIFERA
(SEA SPONGES)

THERE ARE AROUND 5,000 SPECIES OF SEA SPONGES. SOME ARE CARNIVOROUS AND TRAP AND EAT SMALL CRUSTACEANS.

DOMAIN: EUKARYOTA
KINGDOM: ANIMALIA
PHYLUM: PORIFERA

Most animals have specialized tissues. For example, a human body has different kinds of cells for skin, bones, nerves, and so on. Sponges, however, are the most primitive animals, and most of the cells in their bodies don't have specialized jobs. For that reason, it's sometimes possible to tear a sponge in half without killing it. It often simply becomes two sponges.

The sponge's skeleton is usually made of protein fibers. It may also include tiny mineral grains. The flesh itself is like a thin layer of jelly between two layers of cells. Threading through the flesh are many passages that allow ocean water to flow through. Most sponges feed on plankton they filter from the water.

In a few kinds of sponges, the skeleton is so soft and flexible that it can be used as a tool for cleaning. Decades ago, humans took so many sponges for this purpose that these kinds are now rare. The "sponges" we now use are mostly synthetic. Most members of the phylum have harder skeletons that resemble the corals. These are the collectible kinds. They come in a variety of colors. They can also come in an amazing variety of shapes because sponges have no symmetry. For example, one species is called the orange elephant ear because it's often wide and flat, but it can also grow into the shape of a tube or simply lie like rust on a coral reef.

WHERE TO FIND Sponges can be found throughout the world's oceans, from the poles to the tropics. They prefer calm, clear water, as a large amount of sediment would block the pores they use for feeding.

PART THREE

PLAN

{THE PLANT KINGDOM}

NTAE

Magnoliophyta • Pinophyta
Ginkgophyta • Lycophyta

CHAPTER SIX

DIVISIONS

MAGNOLIOPHYTA, PINOPHYTA, GINKGOPHYTA, AND LYCOPHYTA

Most plants produce food through a chemical process called photosynthesis. The main source of energy in this process is sunlight. The raw materials of photosynthesis are carbon dioxide and water. Using light energy, the plant recombines the molecules of water and carbon dioxide into more complicated compounds called carbohydrates. Sugars are examples of carbohydrates. Carbohydrates are rich in energy, which plants can use to fuel their life processes, such as growth and reproduction. Animals can use this energy for the same purposes after they eat the plants—or eat other animals who eat the plants. Some of the energy is passed up the food chain with each meal. In making carbohydrates, the plant also frees up oxygen. Plants, animals, and other living things need oxygen to breathe. The plants make far more than they need.

The major groupings of plants are called divisions, rather than phyla. There are about twelve divisions among the living plants, plus a few more we know from fossil evidence. The classification of plants is in flux because scientists have recently made great progress with genetic evidence. This progress has caused them to discard some of the old categories in favor of more complex systems. Perhaps 90 percent of the plants in the world—and most of the collectible ones—fall into the division flowering plants, or Magnoliophyta. For that reason, we'll concentrate our attention there. A few examples from other divisions appear at the end of this chapter.

MAGNOLIOPHYTA
(FLOWERING PLANTS)

This division is sometimes called by its old name, Angiospermae. Under any name, it covers the flowering plants, the most diverse and successful kind of plants on earth.

Flowers are the reproductive organs of these plants. Many of them make tiny, dustlike particles called pollen. When pollen is taken to another flower, it fertilizes the female reproductive cells it encounters there. The pollen may travel on the wind. It may also be moved by bees, butterflies, and other animals.

Besides the flowers themselves, flowering plants generally produce fruit. The fruit forms from the ovule, or egg-containing capsule, of a flower. Fruit is attractive to animals because it's edible, of course. But why does the plant spend its energy making food for animals? The answer lies in what the animals do besides eating the fruit. Since plants don't typically move around, they need methods of dispersing their seeds so that the offspring don't have to compete with their parents for space and soil. Typically, an animal spreads the seeds it finds in the fruit. It can do this in many ways. For example, a crow may fly away with a piece of fruit, causing its seeds to fall in soil far away from the parent plant. Or an animal might swallow the seeds along with the fruit, then pass them in its feces wherever it happens to travel.

Flowering plants aren't the only kind of plants that reproduce using seeds. However, their seeds differ from those of other plants because they contain an endosperm, which is a packet of nutrition inside the seed to help the embryonic plant grow.

EUDICOTS

Flowering plants fall into several classes. Most of them—more than 70 percent—belong to the class Eudicots. The trait that unites the members of this group is microscopic. On a grain of pollen belonging to a eudicot, there are three small pores hidden in the furrows. Other flowering plants only have one such pore. Another trait eudicots share is having two cotyledons. Cotyledons are the leaves an embryonic plant has even before it germinates. The eudicots include sunflowers, cabbage, and most of the familiar trees.

Painted Dandelion Puff
(*Taraxacum officinale*)

DOMAIN: EUKARYOTA
KINGDOM: PLANTAE
DIVISION: MAGNOLIOPHYTA
CLASS: MAGNOLIOPSIDA
ORDER: ASTERALES
FAMILY: ASTERACEAE
GENUS: *Taraxacum*
SPECIES: *T. officinale*

Each seed-bearing plant has evolved to make sure some of its seeds end up in good patches of soil where they can grow.

The seeds of the dandelion spread on parachutes made of fluffy fibers. The dandelion grows a tall stalk where one of its flowers used to be. The stalk holds the seeds high so the wind can blow them away.

A great way to preserve a dandelion puff is to use clear acrylic spray or hair spray. It not only hardens the fragile parts that would ordinarily blow away, but it thickens those tiny fibers so there's more to look at. This absolutely needs to be done outdoors, though. And be careful to spray gently at least 10 inches from the dandelion, or the force of the spray itself will disperse the fibers. Start with a short, gentle blast of paint. Let it dry. Then apply again as needed.

By the way, "dandelion" comes from the French words for "lion's tooth," *dent de lion*. It got that name because its leaves are ragged, like mouths full of teeth.

WHERE TO FIND Common dandelions are found in temperate regions around the world, especially on lawns and by roadsides.

Dried Lavender
(*Lavandula angustifolia*)

DOMAIN: EUKAROTA
KINGDOM: PLANTAE
DIVISION: MAGNOLIOPHYTA
CLASS: MAGNOLIOPSIDA
ORDER: LAMIALES
FAMILY: LAMIACEAE
GENUS: *Lavandula*
SPECIES: *L. angustifolia*

Common lavender is a popular shrub because of its many uses. It makes a good decoration for yards because of its flowers. They grow on stems separate from the ones that hold the narrow leaves. Each flower stem ends with spikes containing many smaller flowers. Typically, the flowers are light purple. Many people find their scent pleasing. For that reason, lavender is used in perfumes and soaps. Some insects, such as clothes moths, find the scent repugnant; people use the flowers with stored clothes to protect them from the moth's larvae. Lavender is also used in medicine, tea, and even massage oil.

To dry lavender, cut a bunch, leaving about 8 to 10 inches of stem if possible. Gather them all together and bundle them with a rubber band toward the bottom of the bunch. Hang your bunch upside down in a warm, dry room—preferably one that's dark. A closet would work well but only if it's large enough to allow a lot of air to circulate. Drying flowers requires air. Let the lavender hang that way for anywhere between one and four weeks.

WHERE TO FIND Though common lavender is native to the western Mediterranean region, it can be found in gardens worldwide.

Varnished Rose
(genus *Rosa*)

DOMAIN: EUKARYOTA
KINGDOM: PLANTAE
DIVISION: MAGNOLIOPHYTA
CLASS: MAGNOLIOPSIDA
ORDER: ROSALES
FAMILY: ROSACEAE
SUBFAMILY: ROSOIDEAE
GENUS: *Rosa*

Roses are famous for their beauty and their scent. With more than 100 species and many breeds and hybrids, roses can come in almost any color and many sizes. The plant itself can grow in many shapes, too—for example, it can spread like a bush or climb like a vine. Along the woody stems of most roses are prickles shaped like the claws of a cat. The prickles help the rose climb by sticking to fences, tree trunks, and other surfaces. Climbing helps the rose rise above the competition; in a crowded area, tall plants get the best exposure to sunlight.

To dry a rose, prune the parts of the stem that can prick you and leave it as smooth as possible. Cut the stem about 8 to 10 inches from the flower. Tie a string to the very end, and then hang it upside down in a warm, dry room for anywhere between one and four weeks. Roses retain their scent even when dried.

After your rose is quite dry, you might want to spray it with clear spray paint to give it some durability. Without it, the dried flower may not last in your collection for too long.

WHERE TO FIND There are more than one hundred species of roses across the world, and many are not difficult to find. Most regions have naturally occurring species, and roses are often spread beyond their native areas.

Pressed Daisy
(*Bellis perennis*)

DOMAIN: EUKARYOTA
KINGDOM: PLANTAE
DIVISION: MAGNOLIOPHYTA
CLASS: MAGNOLIOPSIDA
ORDER: ASTERALES
FAMILY: ASTERACEAE
GENUS: *Bellis*
SPECIES: *B. perennis*

The common daisy looks like a flower—but it's really hundreds of flowers. In the center of the daisy are tiny yellow flowers packed close together. Around the edges of this cluster are what look like white petals. In fact, these petals are also individual flowers. This structure, in which many small flowers seemingly form a large one, is called a pseudanthium. In the case of the daisy, the whole pseudanthium is held up on a tall stalk called a rachis (the same term used for the central spine of a feather).

To press a daisy, or any flower for that matter, fold a piece of heavyweight paper in half. Watercolor paper is great for this, but even regular printer paper works fine. Carefully place your flower in between the two halves, and press down gently until you've flattened out the leaves. It's not necessary to make them totally flat.

Find an encyclopedia or an old heavy book and place the folded piece of paper with your daisy inside it somewhere in the middle of the book. Wrap the book with strong string or rope. Keep the string taut so the book is really closed tight. Use a pencil as a tourniquet to tighten the string every few days or so. Do this for at least a few weeks, and you'll have a beautiful dried flower for your collection.

WHERE TO FIND The common daisy is native to western, central, and northern Europe, but is widespread in the Americas.

Devil's Claw Seed Pod
(genus *Harpagophytum*)

DOMAIN: EUKARYOTA
KINGDOM: PLANTAE
DIVISION: MAGNOLIOPHYTA
CLASS: MAGNOLIOPSIDA
ORDER: LAMIALES
FAMILY: PEDALIACEAE
GENUS: *Harpagophytum*

A bull grazes on dry grassland. Its hoof catches on a strange object lying on the ground. It looks like a hand with two long, skinny fingers, but it's made of wood. The bull walks on, not even noticing the object. The curved fingers keep it attached to the hoof for hours. Once in a while, the bull's steps knock it against the ground. When that happens, a black seed falls out of an opening between the fingers. Each seed is the size of a small human tooth. The bull may walk for miles before the object falls off. By that time, it has had the chance to spread a dozen or more seeds.

This "hand" is a seed pod called a devil's claw. The devil's claw grows on the unicorn plant. It's the plant's way of spreading seeds. In the spring, the unicorn plant looks like your average weed. Its leaves are dark green and slightly fuzzy, and its branches trail along the ground. If you handle this bad-smelling plant, it will make your hands sticky. That sticky coating is so strong it sometimes traps and kills insects that try to eat the plant.

As the summer sets in, the unicorn plant grows flowers that look like floppy trumpets. Many people grow the unicorn plant because of these pretty pink or yellow flowers. As a flower withers and drops off, a fruit forms at the tip of the branch where it once was. At first these fruits are round and slightly flat, like many other fruits. However, as they grow, they develop a distinctive shape. They begin to look like teardrops with long, curved necks. Some people think the fruit looks like a horse's head with a single horn. That's why they named this the unicorn plant. People sometimes make pickles out of these fruits.

In the hottest part of the summer, a strange thing happens to the fruit. It begins to harden. Then it sheds its skin. The skin dries out and turns from a soft, dark green to a hard, leathery black. As the skin shrivels, you can see the dark wood beneath. Now the fruit is almost ready to turn into a devil's claw. First it needs to bake in the summer sun. The weather has to stay dry for several days in a row. The dry heat makes the neck split neatly down the middle. If you happen to be nearby when this happens, you can hear the cracking sound. The fruit falls off the plant. Another day or two of dry heat makes the two parts of the neck spread far apart. Now they look like fingers. The fruit has become a devil's claw. It's ready to snag the hoof of a passing animal—or the ankle of a person.

By spreading its seeds across the land, the unicorn plant makes sure its offspring don't have to compete with each other. They will sprout far apart, each rooting for its own water and minerals.

WHERE TO FIND Devil's claw is most common in dry places, such as deserts in southwestern California and Arizona, southern Nevada, western Texas, and northern Mexico.

DEVIL'S CLAW HAS BEEN USED BY NATIVE PEOPLES FOR BASKETMAKING FOR CENTURIES.

Varnished (or Waxed) American Elm Leaf
(Ulmus americana)

DOMAIN: EUKARYOTA
KINGDOM: PLANTAE
DIVISION: MAGNOLIOPHYTA
CLASS: MAGNOLIOPSIDA
ORDER: ROSALES
FAMILY: ULMACEAE
GENUS: *Ulmus*
SPECIES: *U. americana*

Elms of one species or another are common across much of North America, Europe, and Asia. I'll focus on the American elm (*Ulmus americana*), but what I say here will apply to many other species. The American elm has rough bark with deep valleys in its flaking surface. Its flowers have no petals, and you might not recognize them as flowers at all; they look more like brownish blisters on its stems. Its seeds are called samaras. They are encased in a papery, oval wing that allows them to be blown by the wind far from the parent tree. Its leaves have slender veins arranged like the vanes of a feather. They have serrated edges and they taper to a point. The leaf is almost symmetrical, but its two halves are set slightly off-kilter.

An artistic way to preserve the leaves of elms (and many other plants) is to press them, as you do with flowers (see page 151). Another way is to microwave them to dry them out flat. To do this, get two ceramic tiles and some rubber bands. Lay the leaf between two pieces of cardboard or paper towels. Sandwich those between the ceramic tiles, and wrap with a rubber band to secure. Place the ceramic tiles with the leaf inside the microwave, and heat for no more than 30 seconds. Take it out, let it cool, then do it again. The trick is to do this slowly so the leaf will dry flat without cracking. After you've dried your elm leaf, spray it lightly with a layer of clear acrylic spray or varnish. Some craft stores carry products specifically for coating dried flowers and leaves.

You can also cover your leaf in wax to preserve it. First, lay your leaf on wax paper. You may want to dry it flat in the microwave first, but this isn't necessary, as the folds and turns in the leaf look beautiful when waxed. Then melt some beeswax in a small pot. When the wax is completely melted, submerge the leaf in the wax. Be careful. The wax will be very hot. Take the leaf out and place it on the wax paper to cool. The leaves dry quickly. Gently peel the leaf off of the wax paper. If there's any excess wax, you can trim it with scissors.

WHERE TO FIND Elm trees are found in many deciduous forests around the world, and once were frequently used in urban and suburban landscaping in North America and Europe. However, in the latter half of the twentieth century, many elms of North American and European origin were killed off by Dutch elm disease.

Apple Seeds
(genus Malus)

DOMAIN: EUKARYOTA
KINGDOM: PLANTAE
DIVISION: MAGNOLIOPHYTA
CLASS: MAGNOLIOPSIDA
ORDER: ROSALES
FAMILY: ROSACEAE
GENUS: *Malus*

Horses, like many animals, love to eat apples. That's a good thing for apple trees. They spread their seeds by packaging them in a delicious fruit. When horses eat the fruit, they swallow the seeds, too. The seed's smooth, tough coat allows it to pass through the horse's body without being digested. Later, the horse drops the seeds onto the ground with its dung. The seeds might then grow into apple trees.

An old myth warns us that apple seeds are poisonous. They really do contain a tiny dose of a poison called cyanide, but you'd have to crush and eat about ten pounds of seeds to get a dangerous dose.

WHERE TO FIND Various species of apple trees are grown worldwide, and apples can be found in almost every grocery store.

Acorn
(genera Quercus and Lithocarpus)

DOMAIN: EUKARYOTA
KINGDOM: PLANTAE
DIVISION: MAGNOLIOPHYTA
CLASS: MAGNOLIOPSIDA
ORDER: FAGALES
FAMILY: FAGACEAE
GENERA: *Quercus* and *Lithocarpus*

Oak trees are common across North America and parts of Asia. Their hard wood is an excellent building material. The trees themselves typically have lobed leaves, sometimes serrated on the edges. An acorn is the nut of the oak (or of a closely related tree). The nut rests in a cupule—a sort of cap with a scaly texture. The nut itself is smooth. It contains acids called tannins, which give it a bitter taste. For some animals, like horses and cattle, the tannins are mildly toxic. Other animals, like pigs and squirrels, eat acorns freely and suffer no ill effects. Humans can eat acorns only after first soaking them in water several times to remove the tannins.

WHERE TO FIND There are hundreds of species of oak trees, occurring in deciduous forests across the Northern Hemisphere, with the greatest diversity of species occurring in North America.

JOHNNY APPLESEED, WHOSE REAL NAME WAS JOHN CHAPMAN, BECAME AN AMERICAN LEGEND BECAUSE OF HIS EFFORTS TO PLANT APPLE TREES AND ORCHARDS ALONG THE WESTERN FRONTIER OF THE US IN THE EARLY 1800S.

Maple Seed
(genus *Acer*)

DOMAIN: EUKARYOTA
KINGDOM: PLANTAE
DIVISION: MAGNOLIOPHYTA
CLASS: MAGNOLIOPSIDA
ORDER: SAPINDALES
FAMILY: SAPINDACEAE
GENUS: *Acer*

The seed of a maple tree has a papery coating. The coating forms a winglike shape with the seed at one end. When the wind blows the seeds off the tree, they spiral down on their wings. Many of them blow far from the tree before they hit the ground.

You can actually eat maple seeds. Just peel off the papery part. If they taste bitter, boil them for a few minutes. Then try them with butter and salt. Just remember to save one for your cabinet.

WHERE TO FIND There are almost 130 species of maple trees, most of which are native to Asia. There are also several that can be found in Europe, northern Africa, and North America. Very few species are found in the Southern Hemisphere.

Calabash Gourd
(*Lagenaria siceraria*)

DOMAIN: EUKARYOTA
KINGDOM: PLANTAE
DIVISION: MAGNOLIOPHYTA
CLASS: MAGNOLIOPSIDA
SUBCLASS: DILLENIIDAE
ORDER: CUCURBITALES
FAMILY: VIOLALES
GENUS: *Lagenaria*
SPECIES: *L. siceraria*

Who invented the bottle? Plants did. Several plants produce fruit that, when carefully hollowed and dried, can serve as a bottle or canteen. Among these are certain vines of the family Cucurbitaceae. This family includes melons, pumpkins, cucumbers, and squash. It also includes gourds, which, like pumpkins, are fruits with a particularly thick rind. Gourds are often used for decoration as well as drinking vessels. Gourds from the calabash vine can grow into the shapes of old-fashioned glass soda bottles. They can also be long and thin, like a zucchini, or round, like a softball.

WHERE TO FIND The calabash gourd has long been domesticated, though it can still be found growing wild. Because of its long history of cultivation, it can be found in most regions throughout the world, but it is believed to have originated from wild plants in southern Africa.

MAPLE LEAVES ALSO MAKE GREAT COLLECTIBLES.
(SEE PAGES 151 AND 153 FOR DIFFERENT
WAYS TO PRESS AND PRESERVE THEM.)

MONOCOTS

Monocots contain only one cotyledon, or embryonic seed-leaf. Their flowers have three petals or petals in multiples of three (for example, six or nine). Often, their leaves have parallel veins. Familiar monocots include grains such as wheat, rice, and corn; other kinds of grasses, including most of the ones found in lawns; palm trees and banana trees; and certain decorative flowers like lilies and daffodils.

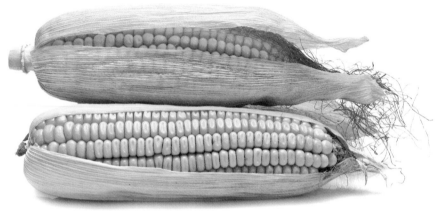

Corn Husk

(Zea mays)

DOMAIN: EUKARYOTA
KINGDOM: PLANTAE
DIVISION: MAGNOLIOPHYTA
CLASS: MAGNOLIOPSIDA
ORDER: CYPERALES
FAMILY: POACEAE
SUBFAMILY: PANICOIDEAE
GENUS: *Zea*
SPECIES: *Z. mays*

Corn, or maize, is a grain widely used for food. The corn plant often grows taller than an adult human. In the wild, it can grow up to 40 feet tall, though it's rare to see a specimen that big.

The leafy stalk gets about as thick as a baseball bat. About every 7 inches, it has a bulbous area called a node; it's like the knuckle on a finger. Leaves grow from each node. The fruit grows above some of the higher nodes on a tuft, which is called an ear. Each ear can contain around six hundred kernels of corn; each kernel is a fruit containing a seed. The kernels are rooted in a hard structure called a cob. The whole ear is protected by specialized leaves called a husk. When the corn is still growing or freshly picked, the husk is flexible and feels like thin, ridged leather. When it dries out, the husk feels like paper, but tougher.

WHERE TO FIND Most people believe that corn originated in Central America. It is now the most widely grown crop in the US and can be found in many regions throughout the world.

WHAT WE OFTEN CALL "BABY" CORN IS ACTUALLY JUST REGULAR CORN HARVESTED EARLY WHILE THE EARS ARE STILL GROWING.

PINOPHYTA
(CONIFERS.)

Several other divisions besides the flowering plants also use seeds for reproduction. Whereas the seeds of flowering plants are clothed in an endosperm, the other kinds have no such packet of nutrition to nourish the embryo. These are "naked seeds," or, to put it in Greek, gymnosperms. Gymnospermae used to be considered a division of the plant kingdom, but scientists have discovered that not all gymnosperms are closely related, so they have placed them in several different divisions.

One of these naked-seed divisions is pinophyta—the conifers. The seeds of a conifer form in a cone. All conifers are woody; most of them are trees, though a few are shrubs. Typically, a conifer grows straight up and has one central trunk. It may ooze resin to protect it from insects. Conifers form huge forests in North America and elsewhere. These forests are the planet's most important recycler of carbon dioxide into food and oxygen.

THERE ARE AROUND SIX HUNDRED CONIFER SPECIES, INCLUDING THE WORLD'S TALLEST AND OLDEST TREES.

Pine Cone (genus *Pinus*)

DOMAIN: EUKARYOTA
KINGDOM: PLANTAE
DIVISION: PINOPHYTA
CLASS: PINOPSIDA
ORDER: PINALES
FAMILY: PINACEAE
GENUS: *Pinus*

Pine trees can grow to 80 feet in height and live for thousands of years. The oldest one now living is believed to be about 4,600 years old. Each year, a pine produces a new ring of branches. Its adult leaves take the form of needles.

Most pine trees produce both male and female cones. The male cones are tiny, usually less than two inches long. They emit pollen and then are shed from the tree. The cones people notice are the female ones, which can grow up to two feet long. They can stay on the tree for years as they mature and then wait for the right time to disperse their seeds. Each cone is made of many scales arranged in a spiral. Each fully developed scale carries two seeds (the scales at the top and bottom of the cone don't fully develop). To disperse its seeds, a cone opens up, spreading its scales apart, and lets the wind blow the seeds away. A few species of pine depend on birds or even forest fires to break open the cones. Since a cone is made of wood, it will last in your cabinet without any special treatment.

WHERE TO FIND Most areas in the Northern Hemisphere have their own native species of pine, but pine trees have been spread outside of their native regions to both temperate and subtropical regions, where they are grown for either timber or decoration.

Sequoia Cone (*Sequoiadendron giganteum*)

DOMAIN: EUKARYOTA
KINGDOM: PLANTAE
DIVISION: PINOPHYTA
CLASS: PINOPSIDA
ORDER: PINALES
FAMILY: CUPRESSACEAE
GENUS: *Sequoiadendron*
SPECIES: *S. giganteum*

Sequoias, also known as redwoods, have been around since Jurassic times, when dinosaurs such as allosaurs and apatosaurs lived. One species called the giant sequoia (*Sequoiadendron giganteum*) is the most massive of all trees, and is the largest known living thing if we measure by volume. The tallest specimen now living stands 311 feet in height. One giant sequoia was so thick that a road was carved through the base of its trunk without killing it.

Another sequoia species, called the California redwood, gets even taller, though it's not as thick. The tallest living California redwood is more than 379 feet high. These trees can get so tall that it's impossible for them to draw enough water through their roots all the way to their tops. They compensate by using aerial roots to absorb fog directly from the air. Part of the reason these trees grow so large is that they live long lives—in one case, 3,500 years.

For such a huge plant, the giant sequoia produces surprisingly small cones, usually less than three inches long. However, a typical tree has eleven thousand cones at a time. The sequoia's life cycle depends on its cone getting damaged: Some of the cones stay closed for decades, hoarding their seeds until a forest fire dries them out and coaxes them open.

WHERE TO FIND The giant sequoia occurs naturally in only one place, the western side of the Sierra Nevada in California.

GINKGOPHYTA

Ginkgo Nut (*Ginkgo biloba*)

DOMAIN: EUKARYOTA
KINGDOM: PLANTAE
DIVISION: GINKGOPHYTA
CLASS: GINKGOOPSIDA
ORDER: GINKGOALES
FAMILY: GINKGOACEAE
GENUS: *Ginkgo*
SPECIES: *G. biloba*

The ginkgo tree (*Ginkgo biloba*) is the only living member of the division ginkgophyta. Its leaves are fan-shaped. Within them, veins run side by side, spreading out as the leaf widens, but never crossing each other. The leaves turn a vivid yellow in the fall and are worth collecting. Even more interesting, though, is the seed.

Unlike conifers, ginkgos don't make cones for their seeds. Instead, two seeds grow from the end of a stalk. Each seed has a hard shell (much like a nut). Outside the shell is a fleshy layer like a fruit. This fleshy layer smells like human vomit or rotting food and it can cause a rash on human skin. You can collect one by wearing gloves. Just squeeze the seed out of the fleshy part, discard the flesh, and then wash the seed thoroughly. You can kill any remaining smell by painting the seed with varnish.

WHERE TO FIND Ginkgo trees are most common in China, though the areas where they are abundant are quite small. The species has also been cultivated in areas of Europe and North America.

LYCOPHYTA

So far we've talked only about plants that reproduce with seeds. Some plants, however, don't produce seeds at all. Instead, they make spores, single cells that can give rise to an entire organism.

One division of spore-bearing plants is the lycophytes. Lycophytes are among the oldest land plants. Fossils show that they have been around for about 410 million years. They differ from most plants in having leaves with only a single vein.

LYCOPHYTES HAVE EXTREMELY
FLAMMABLE SPORES, SO BE CAREFUL
WHERE AND HOW YOU COLLECT THEM!

Resurrection Plant *(Selaginella lepidophylla)*

DOMAIN: EUKARYOTA
KINGDOM: PLANTAE
DIVISION: LYCOPHYTA
CLASS: ISOETOPSIDA
ORDER: SELAGINELLALES
FAMILY: SELAGINELLACEAE
GENUS: *Selaginella*
SPECIES: *S. lepidophylla*

When you first come across a resurrection plant, it may look like nothing but a sloppy gray or brown ball of dead stems. It can be about the size of a man's fist, not counting the tangle of roots dangling from it.

But put the resurrection plant in a dish of water, and something amazing happens. The ball opens up, like a fist unclenching. The gray stems turn green. Leaves unfurl from the stems. In short, it comes to life. This change takes place within a couple of hours.

For centuries, people have used the resurrection plant as a kind of magic trick to amaze others. Really, though, there's nothing magical about it. It is just a plant that adapted to life in the desert. Because deserts get very little rainfall, the plants and animals that live there have to behave differently to survive. For example, cactuses are adapted to desert life. Their thick stems are good at storing water. That trait allows them to live through dry times.

One animal that is good at living in the desert is the harvester ant. It digs its den deep into the soil—10 or 15 feet deep. At that depth, the temperature stays cool and steady. That helps because deserts often have hot days and cold nights. The harvester ant can go inside the den during the hottest part of the day and all of the freezing cold night. It only goes outside when the temperature is right—in the morning, for example.

But what about the resurrection plant? It does well in the desert because it can live through being extremely dried out. It can get so dry it looks dead. When it is dried out, it doesn't do much. Usually, plants take in carbon dioxide from the air and give off oxygen. They use the carbon dioxide, along with sunshine and water, to help them make food for living, growing, and reproducing. You can't see any of this happening, but you can see firm stems and green leaves. None of that happens while the resurrection plant is dried out. It doesn't take in carbon dioxide or give off oxygen or make food. It just lies there looking dead.

But when it rains, the plant opens up and turns green. The plant doesn't need much water. It can turn green just from soaking in the morning dew.

To keep a resurrection plant in your cabinet, all you have to do is dry it out. Take it out of its water dish and don't let it get wet. After a few days, it will curl up into a gray ball. You can put this in your cabinet. When you want to amaze your friends, just take it out and put it in some water again. A resurrection plant can do this trick many times.

WHERE TO FIND *Selaginella lepidophylla* is native to the Chihuahuan Desert. Other types of resurrection plants belonging to a different genus can be found in the deserts of the Middle East.

PART FOUR

MINER

ALIUM

Minerals · Gemstones · Rocks · Fossils

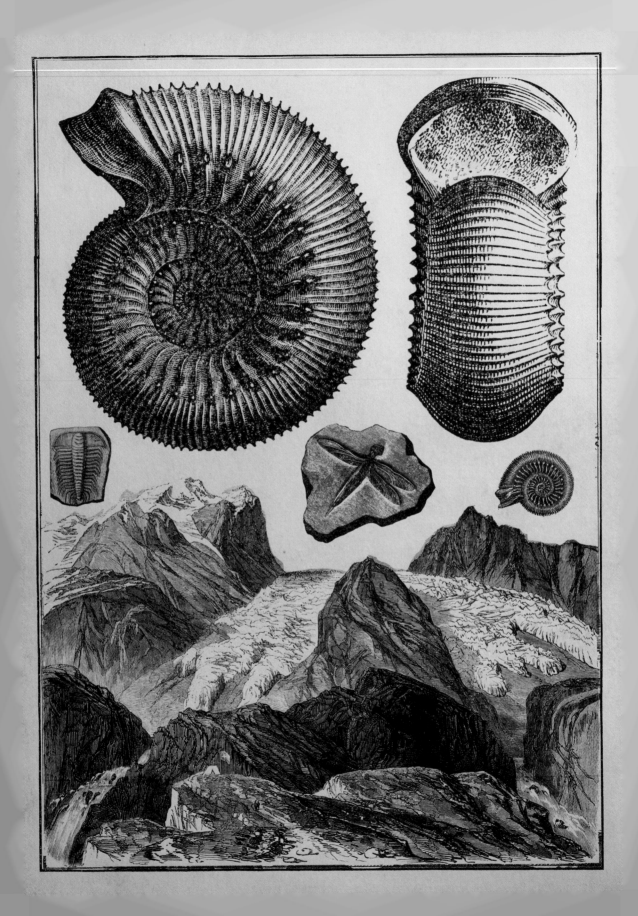

MINERALS, GEMSTONES, AND ROCKS (PLUS FOSSILS)

Is it an animal, vegetable, or mineral? That used to be the first question people would ask when playing guessing games, because that's how Linnaeus divided everything in the world. In his *Imperium Naturae*, Linnaeus stated that there were three kingdoms: Regnum Animale, Regnum Vegetabile, and Regnum Lapideum—otherwise known as the Animal, Vegetable, and Mineral kingdoms. And for many years, that's how people viewed the world. The problem is, scientists no longer use this classification system when it comes to minerals. That being said, while I'm dividing them into their own section in this book, I'm not going to give them taxonomic ranks.

JAMES HUTTON, A SCOTTISH FARMER AND NATURALIST, IS OFTEN CONSIDERED TO BE THE FOUNDER OF MODERN GEOLOGY. HE WAS DRIVEN BY HIS CURIOSITY.

WHAT ARE ROCKS, ANYWAY?

Everybody thinks they know what a rock is...but what is it, exactly? Mostly, a rock is made up of minerals.

But what are minerals?

A mineral is a substance that is made in nature. In order for it to be considered a true mineral, it has to be solid at a certain temperature, and it has to have a specific chemical makeup. Most important, a mineral is made of crystals.

Okay, but what's a crystal?

A crystal is a characteristic geometric shape. If a mineral forms slowly and doesn't get mashed up by something else, it will shape itself into many copies of the same shape. For example, salt—the ordinary kind you can use on food—shapes itself into many little cubes, like playing dice.

Sometimes the shapes within a mineral are too small to see with the naked eye, but a scientist can identify them under a microscope.

Some substances don't count as minerals. Anything made by a plant or animal is not a mineral. For example, bones and shells are made by animals, so they are not minerals. Wood is made by plants. Rubber is made from the sap of certain trees. Those aren't minerals. A tricky one is coal. Coal looks like a black rock, but it's made of things that were once alive (mostly plants), crushed under layers of rock for millions of years. So, it comes from living things and isn't a mineral. Substances made by people don't count as minerals, either.

There are more than 4,900 known mineral species. A mineral with a high concentration of some useful and economically valuable substance, such as iron, is called an ore.

A rock is a chunk of minerals. It can contain just one mineral, or several different ones. If the rock has other stuff mixed in with the minerals, that's okay. It still counts as a rock. A rock's composition is never exact. A rock can be as small as a pebble or as big as a mountain range. The earth's crust is composed of rock. Some rocks have traces of living things in them—animal bones, leaves, even manmade stuff. They're still considered rocks.

A Selection of MINERALS and GEMS

Strictly speaking, a gem is a crystal of a specific material—for example, a diamond. It can be cut and polished to enhance its beauty, and then, perhaps, used in jewelry. However, people often use the term to include pretty rocks that are made up of more than one mineral. For example, a beautiful blue rock called lapis lazuli usually contains at least four different minerals.

Let's start looking at some minerals and rocks that are often considered to be gems. Then we'll look at a few other rocks and minerals that, although not prized for their beauty, have fascinating traits.

Turquoise

Turquoise has been prized for thousands of years and was one of the first gemstones to be mined by humans. It is created when light rainfall dissolves tiny amounts of copper into rock and soil. When the water evaporates, the copper combines with aluminum and phosphorus to create tiny deposits of turquoise. Treasured for its beautiful blue and green hues, turquoise is used almost exclusively for jewelry and art.

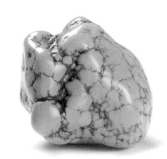

WHERE TO FIND Turquoise is most common in the southwestern US, China, Chile, Egypt, Iran, and Mexico. It is typically found in dry climates and volcanic rock formations.

Fluorite

The word *fluorescent* comes from fluorite, which often produces a blue-violet glow in ultraviolent light. Commonly found as cubic crystals, fluorite has the largest range of colors of any mineral on earth. Fluorite specimens have been found in every color. The most popular varieties are purple. Fluorite is used to create glass, enamel, and special optical lenses.

WHERE TO FIND Fluorite is found worldwide. Particularly large amounts exist in Russia, China, England, France, Spain, Switzerland, India, Morocco, Namibia, South Africa, Canada, Mexico, and the US. An electric-blue variety of fluorite is found exclusively in England.

Serpentine

Named for its green, snakelike color, serpentine is not one mineral but a group of twenty related minerals. Once worn as an amulet to protect wearers against snakes, today the stone is mostly carved for ornamental purposes or used as a replacement for green marble. It is often compared to jade, a similarly green-shaded mineral that is much more valuable.

WHERE TO FIND Serpentine can be found in many places in North America, Europe, Asia, and New Zealand. In the US, large amounts of serpentine come from New York, Pennsylvania, and California, where it is the official state rock.

Quartz

Although the ancient Roman writer Pliny the Elder believed quartz was made of permanently frozen ice, the majority of quartz is actually created from crystallized molten volcanic rock. Quartz specimens can range in color from translucent (occasionally even transparent) to rosy pink and golden yellow. Its gemstone varieties include amethyst and citrine.

WHERE TO FIND Quartz is one of the most common minerals in the earth's crust and can be found in numerous places around the world, most often in sandstone, granite, and shale.

Onyx

A variety of quartz, onyx can be found in many different colors but is most often deep black, red, brown, or black with white bands. Once popular in ancient Greece, Rome, and Egypt, onyx is still considered to be a quite valuable gem.

WHERE TO FIND Because it derives from quartz, onyx can be found nearly everywhere on earth. It is most common in Brazil, East Asia, Madagascar, and the US.

Tiger's Eye

Another derivate of quartz, tiger's eye is a golden, amber-brown gemstone with a bright luster. Considered a semiprecious stone, tiger's eye is used exclusively in art and jewelry. A blue-gray variant is called hawk's eye.

WHERE TO FIND Uncommon worldwide, tiger's eye is mostly found in South Africa. Smaller amounts are located in Namibia, Australia, India, and Thailand.

Jasper

Jasper is an opaque rock and a variety of quartz. It is often brown, yellow, or reddish in color, and is usually spotted or striped. Some types of jasper are banded, but not all types. Banded jasper can look very similar to agate, but unlike agate, it is opaque. Jasper is one of the birthstones for the month of March.

WHERE TO FIND Jasper can be found anywhere in the world. It is especially common in the western US, particularly in the states of Arizona, Utah, Oregon, Idaho, Washington, California, and Texas.

Amethyst

Amethyst, the most valuable variety of quartz, comes in hues that range from nearly transparent to deep purple. The deep purple colors are the most prized. The colors of some amethyst varieties slowly fade over time due to light exposure.

WHERE TO FIND Amethyst exists nearly everywhere but is most abundant in South Africa, South America, North America, and Russia. Colors and shapes vary by location. For example, amethyst from the state of Arizona has a deep purplish-blue color, while amethyst from Russia has reddish highlights.

Agate

Similar to jasper, agate is a banded form of quartz that can be found in a wide variety of colors and textures. Most agate forms by filling a cavity in volcanic rock, so the stones are often round. Agate specimens have such distinctive ring patterns that no two look alike.

WHERE TO FIND Agate is common in Mexico, Argentina, Uruguay, Brazil, India, Australia, and the US, particularly in the states of Oregon, Arizona, Montana, Wyoming, South Dakota, and Michigan.

Magnesite

The mineral magnesite is mostly white with black or brown veins. It has a variety of purposes, from the production of synthetic rubber to use in jewelry and art. In 1984, traces of magnesite were found on a Martian meteorite discovered in Antarctica. Since then, the mineral has also been found on Mars itself.

WHERE TO FIND Most of the world's magnesite is found in Europe, Asia, Australia, and South America.

Gypsum

Soft enough to be scratched with just a tip of a fingernail, and known for its incredible flexibility, gypsum is one of the most widely used minerals in the world. Uses for gypsum range from fertilizer to wall plastering, sheetrock, and the cement used for bridges and highways. Gypsum comes in a range of colors. Its varieties include alabaster, desert rose, and selenite.

WHERE TO FIND Gypsum is extremely common and can be found all around the world. Gypsum crystals have been discovered in caves, clay beds, and occasionally sandy areas like beaches. Exceptional specimens have been found in Central America and the western US.

Fool's Gold (Pyrite)

Lots of rocks are interesting just because of the minerals inside of them—for example, fool's gold.

Fool's gold isn't gold at all. It's really a mineral called pyrite. It gets its name because people often mistake pyrite for gold. It's an easy mistake to make. Both are shiny, yellowish metals. Gold is worth a lot of money. Pyrite isn't worth much at all. It's a common mineral to find in rocks just lying around on the ground.

To tell the difference between the two metals, scientists use the streak test. The streak test is so easy anybody can do it. You just need a flower pot. It must be the ceramic kind. These pots are usually the reddish color of bricks. To do the streak test, you simply scratch your rock against the flower pot. It should leave a streak on the pot. If you have real gold, the streak will be gold-colored. If you have pyrite, the streak will be greenish black.

WHERE TO FIND Pyrite is an extremely common mineral, although its shape often varies—from flat and spherical discs to rough cubes—depending on the location. It's most common in the western and midwestern US, as well as Peru, Spain, Russia, and South Africa.

A WORD ABOUT REAL GOLD (AND COPPER AND SILVER)

GOLD NUGGET: Although it has been discovered on every continent except Antarctica, gold is an exceptionally rare mineral, making it one of the most sought-after metals on earth. Gold in its natural mineral form usually contains silver, copper, and iron. Gold nuggets, however, are made almost entirely of pure gold with a tiny bit of silver mixed in. They are incredibly uncommon, but can be found in stream and riverbeds. Most gold is mined from rock or ore, rather than actual nuggets. The ore is often iron-rich rock or white quartz and contains only the smallest amount of gold. The Atlantic and Pacific Oceans hold the majority of the world's gold supply, containing around eight times the amount of gold mined to date.

COPPER ORE: One of the world's most consumed metals, copper ore is mined from the ground for a variety of purposes, one of which is its use as a powerful conductor of electricity. Compared to gold, pure copper is much more common. Today, Chile holds approximately one third of the world's known supply of copper, which is mostly mined from the Andes Mountains.

SILVER ORE: Silver has been used for ornamental purposes for thousands of years. It is incredibly resistant and much harder to dissolve than many other minerals. Most silver is extracted from silver ores mined from the earth. Pure silver is usually mixed with small amounts of gold, copper, and lead, or combined with other chemical elements like sulfur, arsenic, and chlorine. Like gold, it can be found near riverbeds and streams. More abundant than gold, but still incredibly rare, silver is largely found in North, Central, and South America.

METAMORPHIC ROCKS

Petrologists (people who study rocks) divide rocks into three categories: metamorphic, igneous, and sedimentary. Metamorphic rocks are formed when igneous or sedimentary rocks become transformed by heat or pressure deep inside the earth. They make up a huge percentage of the earth's crust.

Soapstone

Soapstone is a metamorphic rock made up mostly of talc. The softest mineral on earth, talc is often used for sculptures because it is so easily carved. Because soapstone is composed of talc, it is also quite soft. It often even feels like soap, which is where it gets its name. Many cultures have used the rock for various purposes. Some varieties can even be put in the freezer, frozen, and used as ice cubes.

WHERE TO FIND Soapstone can be found everywhere. Much of it comes from Brazil, China, India, Europe, and the US.

Marble

Marble is a metamorphic rock formed from heated and pressurized limestone. It is made mostly of the mineral calcite and contains many other minerals, most often quartz, graphite, and pyrite, or fool's gold. Marble is found in large deposits that can be hundreds of feet thick. It is light in color and mostly white, gray, pink, yellow, or black. The most prized marble is almost pure white. Marble can be crushed or cut into large pieces and polished. It is used in everything from highways to important monuments and sculptures. The Taj Mahal is made completely of marble.

WHERE TO FIND Marble can be found all over the world, but large concentrations occur in the US, Europe, and India.

MARBLE HAS BEEN USED SINCE ANCIENT TIMES FOR SCULPTURES. PURE WHITE MARBLE HAS FEW OR NO STAINS AND IS SOMEWHAT SOFT WHEN FIRST QUARRIED, MAKING IT RELATIVELY EASY TO CARVE AND ONLY HARDENING AFTER TIME. THE SEMI-TRANSLUCENT FINISH ALSO GIVES MARBLE AN ALMOST LIFELIKE APPEARANCE, AS WITH THIS "MEDICI LION" AT THE ENTRANCE OF THE VORONTSOV PALACE IN ALUPKA, UKRAINE.

IGNEOUS ROCKS

Igneous rocks are formed when molten rock material deep inside the earth changes from being a liquid into a solid. Some igneous rocks are formed above the earth's surface when molten rock, in the form of lava, solidifies.

Thunder Egg

Sometimes a rock is fascinating because of the way the different minerals in it are arranged. Hundreds of years ago, people on the western coast of North America noticed something interesting. When certain rocks got broken open, they had beautiful patterns inside. Some of them revealed smooth, pink stone. Others had bright, clear crystals. Some had several colors swirled together. On the outside, these rocks were plain and round. They were only beautiful on the inside.

The people made up stories to explain these special rocks. They said the spirits who supposedly lived in the mountains got mad and threw lightning at each other. Inside each lightning bolt, they said, was one of these special rocks. They called the rocks "thunder eggs."

These days, scientists know how thunder eggs really come to be. They happen when lava erupts from a volcano. Not every volcano makes thunder eggs. Thunder eggs get made when a volcano spits out a type of lava called rhyolite. Rhyolite is thick and gooey. It is made up of several minerals mixed together. The lava cools down after it oozes out of the volcano. As it cools, it hardens into solid rock. The different minerals in the rhyolite don't all cool down at the same speed, though. Some get hard faster than others. That's why you might find a chunk of one mineral inside a chunk of a different kind of mineral. The one inside cooled down first. The outside mineral was still liquid, and it washed all over the inside chunk, then hardened.

There are special saws that can cut smoothly through rock. People often cut open thunder eggs and polish them so they can look at their beautiful insides. These look great in a cabinet.

WHERE TO FIND Thunder eggs can be found all over the world—from lush forests to dry, desert terrains. Oregon is famous for its particular abundance of this rock.

Obsidian

Obsidian is an igneous rock that forms when molten rock is cooled so fast its atoms don't crystalize. Obsidian often solidifies along the edges of a lava flow, volcanic dome, or where lava touches water. It is usually black with a smooth, glassy texture, but it can also be brown, green, and very rarely yellow, orange, or red. Sometimes obsidian will contain a mixture of two of these colors, often black and brown. Obsidian was once popularly used for arrowheads.

WHERE TO FIND Obsidian can be found in many locations with previous volcanic activity. Large amounts are found in South and Central America, Europe, Japan, Indonesia, New Zealand, Russia, and North America. In the US, it is mostly found in Nevada, New Mexico, Arizona, Idaho, Wyoming, Oregon, Washington, and California.

Volcanic Rock

Volcanic rocks are a broad subset of igneous rocks. They are formed when lava erupts from a volcano, cools, and solidifies. Their appearance can vary depending on the type of lava and how fast it cooled. Some volcanic rocks are black and glassy in texture, like obsidian. Others look droplet-shaped or are spongelike, such as pumice. Pumice is created when lava froths into foam. It is so light it can float in the ocean. Pele's hair is a form of volcanic glass formed by winds, which stretch thin strands of hot lava that cool to glass.

WHERE TO FIND Volcanic rocks exist worldwide in areas with past volcanic activity, like Italy, Mexico, France, and in the states of Washington, Arizona, New Mexico, and Hawaii.

SEDIMENTARY ROCKS

Sedimentary rocks don't form beneath the earth, but near the surface, in the earth's oceans, rivers, and deserts. They're formed by layers of mud and sand and other forms of sediment that are buried and then harden into rocks over time. Since the rocks are created as layers, with the oldest layers being on the bottom of the rock, they can tell scientists a lot about the earth's history by their composition.

Chalk

Chalk is a variety of limestone (see page 175). It is made from the calcite shells of microorganisms called coccolithophores. These microbes live in the ocean. When one of them dies, it drifts down to the ocean floor. Scavengers and decay remove most of the body, but the shell remains. Over the centuries, trillions of these microscopic shells accumulate on the ocean floor. The weight of the sediment and water on top of them eventually compresses them into stone, which we call chalk. The white cliffs of Dover, England, are famously made from chalk.

WHERE TO FIND Chalk deposits are found in many parts of the world, including the US, Egypt, Israel, Australia, and much of northwestern Europe.

Flint

Flint is a sedimentary rock form of quartz. It often occurs in layers of chalk beds and other types of limestone. Flint does not have a specific color, but it is usually gray, white, black, or brown. A piece of flint can be struck with iron or steel to create a spark, and its razor-sharp edge made it a popular tool in ancient times. To make sure you've really found a piece of flint, strike it against a piece of steel or iron to see if it sparks.

WHERE TO FIND Flint can be found all over the world. Because of erosion, it is often found near freshwater creeks, riverbeds, and lakeshores.

Limestone

Some rocks are fun to collect because of what you can do with them. Limestone is an example.

Limestone is made partly of the skeletons and shells of animals that live in water. When the animals die, their shells are left behind and they slowly dissolve. The shells are made up mostly of calcium carbonate. Some of the calcium settles out of the water but most of it lands on the bottom of the sea floor. Most of the calcium carbonate bits are too small to see. But when millions of the bits pile up together, they make a fine, sandlike sediment. Mixed in with this sediment are bigger chunks of shell. Sometimes even whole shells get mixed in. They don't dissolve because they get buried in the sediment. Billions of sea animals die over thousands of years. Their remains pile up into deep beds of sediment.

But how does this sediment turn into stone? *Pressure* is the answer. Pressure happens because a lot of weight lies on top of the sediment. Some of the weight comes from the water. Water is heavier than it looks. You can see this for yourself. Take an empty milk jug. Notice how light it is. Then fill it up with water and carry it around for a minute. Pretty heavy, right? Now imagine being at the bottom of the sea, with miles of water above you. That would be a lot of pressure. In fact, people can't go very deep in the water because of the pressure. Even with SCUBA gear to help them breathe, people can only go about 400 feet down—and only people with special training can manage that depth.

Some of the weight comes from other stuff that falls on top of the sediment, like sand or just more calcium sediment. Thousands of years of pressure squeeze the water out of the sediment and crunch its pieces together tightly. That's how it becomes limestone.

There's a neat trick you can do with limestone. Pour a tiny amount of vinegar onto it. You will see the stone fizz up. That's because a chemical reaction is going on. The vinegar contains a mild acid that eats into the limestone.

WHERE TO FIND You can find limestone anywhere in the world where large amounts of sedimentary rock have been exposed by erosion and other forces.

SPACE ROCKS

Everyone knows about the planets orbiting our sun—Mercury, Venus, Mars, Jupiter, Saturn, Uranus, Neptune, and of course Earth. There are other items circling the sun as well. Asteroids are minor planets, often rocky, mostly circling within the orbit of Jupiter. Comets are similar bodies that carry significant amounts of ice. Typically their orbits are eccentric. They don't travel in a circle around the sun, but in a lopsided ellipse. As they approach the sun, the radiation turns their ice into a visible halo of gas. Some of it may trail behind the comet as a tail. Many other bodies similar to asteroids and comets orbit the sun. Ones smaller than a meter, yet bigger than a grain, are called meteoroids. Sometimes meteoroids fly into the earth's atmosphere. Their disintegration in the air may produce a bright streak of light. This is called a meteor, or, informally, a shooting star. If the object reaches the ground, it's called a meteorite.

The earth is constantly being pelted by these space rocks, although most of them burn up before they reach the ground, or disappear into the ocean. But over the years, more than forty thousand meteorites have been found by scientists and self-described "meteor hunters." Some are the size of tiny pebbles, but some have been quite large. Although any rocks found in public parks belong to the government, and any rocks found on private property belong to the owner of the property, there are vast portions of public lands in the American West where ownership of meteorites is questionable. This varies from region to region. If you decide to look for meteorites on your own, you should check what the rules and regulations are in that region. Be forewarned: Your chances of finding a meteorite are pretty slim. These alien stones are more rare than gold—or even diamonds. If I could look anywhere in the world for meteorites, I'd start with either a desert, like the Mojave, or a place covered in ice. The light surface areas provide great contrast for spotting meteorites, which are usually black or dark gray. In the case of deserts, another reason they make ideal meteorite-hunting spots is that their surfaces haven't been washed away by centuries of rainfall. In fact, they're likely to have been exposed and little-changed for thousands of years.

A vital instrument for any meteor hunter is a metal detector. The iron and nickel in many meteorites will set off a good metal detector, and make finding them by eye a little easier. It's also a quick way to tell the difference between a regular rock and a space rock. Some meteorites contain so much iron, they'll stick to a magnet.

Meteorites

Meteorites are pieces of rock that have fallen from space. This sometimes happens when two asteroids collide. Sometimes meteorites come from the moon, or Mars, as a result of an asteroid collision on one of those celestial bodies. Either way—whether they were created by asteroids, which would make them as old as our solar system (more than 4.5 billion years old), or created on a neighboring planet, which might make them a little younger—they are literally a piece of the cosmos.

There are three types of meteorites: stony meteorites, which are mostly made of stone; iron meteorites, which are mostly iron and nickel; and stony-iron, which have a some of both. The most common meteorites are actually the stony kind, but since they look more like common rocks, they are often left alone, unrecognized. Iron meteorites are easier to identify and locate, because of their magnetic qualities, so they are more frequently encountered in collections. Some meteorites even contain gemstones like crystals and diamonds.

Most meteorites are small enough to collect, but there have been many big enough to leave impact craters. One leading theory about the extinction of the dinosaurs is that it was caused by the impact of a huge meteorite in the Yucatán peninsula, which spread a cloud of superheated dust across the region, blocking out the sun. There would have been massive fires, as well as earthquakes and tsunamis, in such a cataclysmic event.

Some stone meteorites, like this example to the left, are easy to overlook because they look like ordinary earth rocks. Iron meteorites, like the one above, are easier to identify with the naked eye. If you do find a meteorite on your own, be sure to check in with scientists before putting it in your cabinet of curiosities. They may be able to help you get some information about your meteorite, and they may also be able to use data recovered about the piece to help them with their quest to catalog the cosmos.

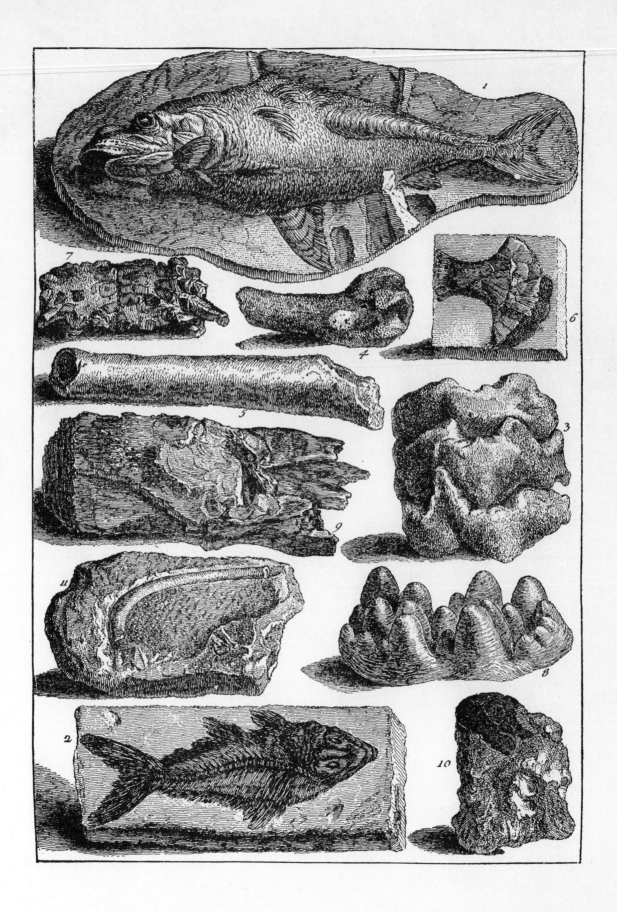

FOSSILS (AND PREHISTORIC RELICS)

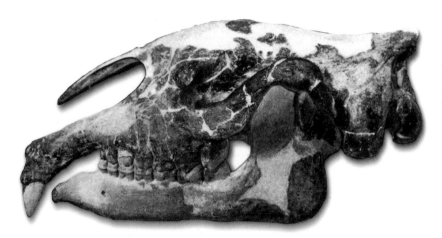

This skull belongs to the Paraceratherium, an extinct relative of the rhinoceros and the largest mammal—at more than 16 feet tall—to have ever walked the earth.

Living things leave many kinds of traces. For example, we know a lot about prehistoric life because of the footprints prehistoric creatures left behind. Their footprints got preserved when these animals walked in mud, which then hardened into rock. This is just one type of fossil. Another kind of fossil is bone. Most bones are slowly destroyed by scavengers, weather, decay, or erosion, but sometimes a bone or even an entire skeleton will turn up in rocks. The most famous bone finds are, of course, dinosaurs, but many other animals have been preserved as well. For example, an expedition led by the naturalist Roy Chapman Andrews in 1922 discovered a leg bone taller than a man. It belonged to a Paraceratherium, a gigantic extinct mammal related to the rhinoceros.

The men and women who discover and study fossils are called paleontologists. They search all around the world looking for fossils and dig them out of rocks with tools such as a hammer or chisel. Fossils can be found anywhere, sometimes even in the most unexpected places. The remains of prehistoric sea creatures have been found in areas without any water nearby, even in the highest places on the planet like the Himalayas. This tells scientists that long ago the mountains were completely under water.

The best place to find any sort of fossil is where sedimentary rocks like limestone are exposed. This is most common on beaches or in rock quarries. While fossils often need to be dug out of rock, many might be hiding in plain sight.

Trilobite (class Trilobita)

KINGDOM: ANIMALIA
PHYLUM: ARTHROPODA
CLASS: TRILOBITA

Trilobites are some of the oldest fossils around. They date back to the Paleozoic Era, 240 to 520 million years ago. Scientists believe they may be related to crustraceans and insects.

WHERE TO FIND Trilobites have been found on every continent in the world in various locations, from the Himalayas in southern Asia to Death Valley in the Mojave Desert.

Ammonite
(class Cephalopoda)

KINGDOM: ANIMALIA
PHYLUM: MOLLUSCA
CLASS: CEPHALOPODA

Ammonites are anywhere between 65 and 240 million years old. They are the prehistoric remains of long extinct, squidlike sea creatures, usually with flat, spiral shell shapes. Ammonites come in all different sizes. Some are as small as a fingernail while others are as large as 2 or 3 feet wide.

WHERE TO FIND Ammonites are among the most abundant types of fossils found today.

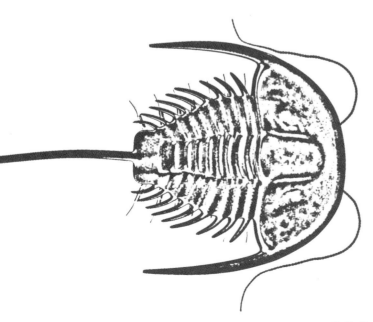

TRILOBITES LIVED FOR MORE THAN 300 MILLION YEARS, BUT WERE ONE OF THE MANY CASUALTIES OF THE PERMIAN MASS EXTINCTION EVENT, WHICH CAUSED THE END OF MOST MARINE SPECIES AT THE TIME. THE CLOSEST LIVING RELATIVE TO TRILOBITES ARE HORSESHOE CRABS.

Fossil Fish

Known as the Age of Fish, the Devonian period is famous for the incredible number of fish species that developed more than 400 million years ago. Many of these new fish species had powerful jaws and sharp teeth. They are ancestors of modern sharks and rays. Fossils dating from the Devonian period can be found in rocks and lake basins all over the world. Bony fish are the most commonly preserved.

WHERE TO FIND Fish fossils are common in both fresh and salt water all over the world. The Rocky Mountains are one of the world's best locations for finding fossil fish.

THE COELACANTH IS KNOWN AS A "LIVING FOSSIL" BECAUSE, FOR MANY YEARS, IT WAS KNOWN ONLY FROM FOSSILS. THEN, IN 1938, A FISHERMAN FISHED A LIVE COELACANTH FROM THE WATERS OFF SOUTH AFRICA. THIS SPECIES IS APPROXIMATELY 400 MILLION YEARS OLD!

Amber and Resin

The fossilized resin of prehistoric plants is called amber. Resin is a sticky fluid a plant uses to discourage bugs and other animals from eating it. Sometimes, mosquitoes or other insects get trapped in the resin, which preserves them for hundreds of thousands or even millions of years. That's because the resin eventually hardens into amber with the mosquitoes still inside it. This counts as two kinds of fossil: First, the amber itself is a fossil because it was part of the living tree. Second, the mosquitoes are now fossils, because the amber preserves them. Amber is most often a deep orange red or yellow. A rare blue form of amber exists only in the Dominican Republic.

WHERE TO FIND Amber can be found all over the world, particularly in Europe, Asia, and the Americas. It is often torn from the seafloor and washed up on shore.

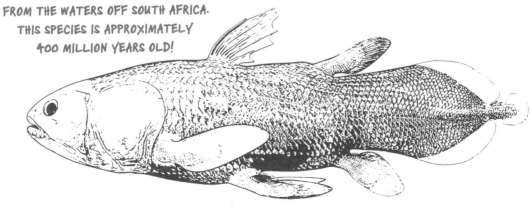

CURIO

SITIES

curiosity, n.

1. A strong desire to see something novel, or to discover something unknown, either by research or inquiry; a desire to gratify the senses with a sight of what is new or unusual, or to gratify the mind with new discoveries; inquisitiveness.

2. Nicety; delicacy.

3. Accuracy; exactness; nice performance; curiousness; as the curiosity of workman—ship.

4. A nice experiment; a thing unusual or worthy of curiosity.

5. An object of curiosity; that which excites a desire of seeing, or deserves to be seen, as novel and extraordinary.

—From the 1828 edition of *Noah Webster's American Dictionary of the English Language*

CURIOSITIES

The natural world is full of too many beautiful and strange wonders to include them all in this book. Rather than having quelled your curiosity about these wonders, my hope is that this book has awakened it even more. We are in an age of specialization, where people tend to focus on one career or have one area of expertise, but there's a little bit of the polymath in everyone. We're all explorers, conservationists, and collectors by nature. Collecting souvenirs of our world is just one way of appreciating its beauty. Cataloging these tokens brings a little order to its chaotic wildness. Wisdom comes from learning about them, from the tiniest creatures in our collections to the relics of the past.

Every time you fill your cabinet with one more curiosity, you're adding a connection between you and the tremendous biodiversity around you—which you're both a part of, and a witness to. You also become part of a long history of humans endeavoring to preserve and remember the past. Had it not been for the curiosity of some collectors and artists a few hundred years ago, we might never have known about the dinosaurs. Had it not been for the curiosity of the paleontologists and botanists and explorers of earlier times, we might still believe that ammonites are petrified snakes and the skulls of woolly rhinoceroses are the evidence of dragons. Human beings are inherently full of curiosity. It's what's allowed us to grow as a species, and what's given us the ability to understand life around us. It's what's allowed us to see our place on earth, how we're just one species of a genus in a family in the primate order of mammals in the Chordate phylum of the animal kingdom.

Have fun collecting!

ACKNOWLEDGMENTS

I'm indebted to the many editors, photographers, designers, and production people who brought this book to life, especially Raquel Jaramillo, who conceived and designed the project and brought me aboard as the writer.

In collecting natural wonders, I've had wonderful help from Tracy, Parker, Beckett, and Griffin. Many thanks also to D'Arcy Allison-Teasley, who lent me some of her own treasures to write about.

ABOUT THE AUTHOR

Gordon Grice is the author of *The Red Hourglass: Lives of the Predators*, *The Book of Deadly Animals*, and the National Geographic ebook *Shark Attacks*. His articles about wildlife and biology have appeared in *The New Yorker*, *Harper's*, and *Discover*. He lives in Wisconsin and online at gordongrice.com.

PHOTO AND ART CREDITS

10-15